BENJAMIN
FRANKLIN
SCIENTIST AND STATESMAN

SPECIAL LIVES IN HISTORY THAT BECOME

BENJAMIN

FRANKLIN

SCIENTIST AND STATESMAN

by Brenda Haugen
and Andrew Santella

Content Adviser: Richard J. Bell,
History Department, Harvard University

Reading Adviser: Rosemary G. Palmer, Ph.D.,
Department of Literacy, College of Education,
Boise State University

COMPASS POINT BOOKS MINNEAPOLIS, MINNESOTA

Compass Point Books
3109 West 50th Street, #115
Minneapolis, MN 55410

Visit Compass Point Books on the Internet at *www.compasspointbooks.com*
or e-mail your request to *custserv@compasspointbooks.com*

Editor: Jennifer VanVoorst
Lead Designer: Jaime Martens
Photo Researcher: Svetlana Zhurkina
Page Production: Heather Griffin
Cartographer: XNR Productions, Inc.
Educational Consultant: Diane Smolinski

Managing Editor: Catherine Neitge
Art Director: Keith Griffin
Production Director: Keith McCormick
Creative Director: Terri Foley

To Todd McCord. Thank you for all your support and encouragement.
I love you! BLH

Library of Congress Cataloging-in-Publication Data
Haugen, Brenda.
  Benjamin Franklin : scientist and statesman / by Brenda Haugen and
Andrew Santella.
     p. cm. — (Signature lives)
  Includes bibliographical references and index.
  ISBN-13: 978-0-7565-0826-5 (hardcover)
  ISBN-10: 0-7565-0826-6 (hardcover)
  ISBN-13: 978-0-7565-1072-5 (paperback)
  ISBN-10: 0-7565-1072-4 (paperback)
  1. Franklin, Benjamin, 1706-1790—Juvenile literature. 2. Statesmen—
United States—Biography—Juvenile literature. 3. Scientists—United
States—Biography—Juvenile literature. 4. Inventors—United States—
Biography—Juvenile literature. 5. Printers—United States—Biography—
Juvenile literature. I. Santella, Andrew. II. Title. III. Series.
E302.6.F8H37 2005
973.3'092—dc22   2004023194

Signature Lives

REVOLUTIONARY WAR ERA

The American Revolution created heroes—and traitors—who shaped the birth of a new nation: the United States of America. "Taxation without representation" was a serious problem for the American colonies during the mid-1700s. Great Britain imposed harsh taxes and didn't give the colonists a voice in their own government. The colonists rebelled and declared their independence from Britain—the war was on.

1 BENJAMIN FRANKLIN'S RETURN

∾∿∾

The news quickly spread through the busy streets of Philadelphia. Benjamin Franklin was coming home. It was 1775, and Philadelphia's favorite son had been in England for nearly 18 years. Now he was returning home at a time when he was badly needed. A huge crowd gathered to welcome their city's hero. Franklin's daughter, Sarah Bache, and her family led the way. Franklin had never seen Sarah's youngest son, also named Benjamin, who was now about 6 years old. Franklin had missed so much while he was away.

Arriving in Philadelphia on May 5, 1775, Franklin found his city buzzing with talk of war and rebellion. For years, American colonists had been complaining that Great Britain's government was not treating

In his lifetime, Benjamin Franklin was successful in many fields, including printing, science, and politics.

In 1775, British troops clashed with American volunteer soldiers called Minutemen in Lexington, Massachusetts.

them fairly. Finally, the colonists' angry protests turned into violent conflict. In April, British soldiers and American militia clashed in bloody battles in Massachusetts. In Philadelphia and throughout the 13 colonies, people prepared for war.

Franklin had hoped the British and the American colonists could work out their differences peacefully. He had many close friends in Britain. To him, the city of London felt almost as much like home as Philadelphia. Even so, now that war had arrived, Franklin embraced the American cause.

The day after Franklin returned to Philadelphia, he was elected to represent Pennsylvania in the Second Continental Congress. Later he negotiated France's help in the war against Great Britain. Franklin's work played an important part in securing American independence.

Franklin was 69 years old when he returned home to Philadelphia. He had already lived a full life. He had built a successful printing business, making himself wealthy in the process. His inventions and experiments with electricity had won him fame and respect. He could have retired and rested, secure in his fame. He could have spent more time with his family, which was something he had sacrificed in order to serve his fellow colonists. Instead, Franklin jumped into the fight for freedom. He still had important work to do.

Because of his work in the diverse fields of science, literature, and politics, and his expertise in trades such as printing and candle-making, Benjamin Franklin is often called America's Renaissance Man. This title refers to a time period in Europe—the 14th–16th centuries—when artists such as Leonardo da Vinci were skilled in many different areas.

Chapter 2 BOSTON BOYHOOD

⤫⤬⤫

Long before he began working for American independence, the young Benjamin Franklin displayed an independent streak of his own. He spent much of his childhood struggling against the wishes of his father.

Benjamin Franklin was born in Boston, Massachusetts, on a cold, blustery Sunday—January 17, 1706. Though they didn't have much money, the Franklin family was rich with love. Ben's father, Josiah Franklin, had come to Boston from England in 1683. He made soap and candles for a living. Ben's mother, Abiah Folger, married Josiah after the death of Josiah's first wife. With wives from two marriages, Josiah fathered a total of 17 children. Ben, the youngest son, was the 15th child.

When Benjamin Franklin was a boy, Boston was a busy shipping port and the largest city in North America.

Being one of the youngest children, Ben quickly learned to use his wits rather than force to get his way. His older siblings not only outweighed him, they outnumbered him.

They were also quick to point out any mistake Ben might make. One lesson they taught him involved the value of money and how wasting it makes a person look foolish. When Ben was 7, some friends gave him money as a gift. Years later, Ben remembered:

> *I went directly to a shop where they sold toys for children, and being charmed with the sound of a whistle that I met by the way, in the hands of another boy, I voluntarily offered and gave all my money for it. When I came home, whistling all over the house, much pleased with my whistle, but disturbing all the family, my brothers, sisters and cousins, understanding the bargain I had made, told me I had given four times as much for it as it was worth, put me in mind of what good things I might have bought with the rest of the money, and laughed at me so much for my folly that I cried with vexation; and the reflection gave me more chagrin than the whistle gave me pleasure. ... As I came into the world, and observed the actions of men, I thought I met many who gave too much for the whistle.*

Benjamin Franklin was born in this home on Milk Street in Boston, Massachusetts.

The Franklin home buzzed with activity. Josiah often invited educated people to share his family's simple evening meals. Josiah wanted his children to benefit from hearing intelligent conversation. Music often filled the Franklin household, too. With his beautiful voice, Josiah sang hymns in the evening while playing the violin. Ben inherited Josiah's love of music and learned to play the violin, harp, guitar, and other instruments.

Ben also loved the sea. He grew up just a short walk away from Boston Harbor. Boston was then the busiest seaport in North America, with ships

> *Ben was named after his uncle Benjamin, Josiah's favorite brother. For many years, Uncle Benjamin continued to live in England. When Ben was old enough to read and write, he borrowed Josiah's ink-well and quill pen and wrote many long letters to Uncle Benjamin. Ben always enjoyed writing to adults.*

from around the world making regular stops there.

Ben spent many of his early days playing along the Boston waterfront. He learned to swim and handle small boats when he was still very young. He made a pair of wooden flippers and hand paddles to help himself swim better. One day, he used a kite to catch the wind and pull himself across a pond as he floated in the water.

Ben was a leader among his friends, and he often came up with ideas for projects that involved them, too. Sometimes his ideas got them all into trouble, though. Once, the boys got tired of standing on the boggy soil at their favorite fishing pond. When Ben spied a pile of rocks set aside to build the foundation of a house, he got an idea. He told his friends to meet him back at the pond that evening.

When evening came, the boys arrived as promised. Ben and his friends collected the pile of rocks and made a dock out of them. Now they could fish in comfort without getting wet.

In the morning, the house builders saw what had happened to their rocks and were hopping mad. When they discovered the identities of the boys, the builders went to talk to the boys' parents.

Josiah confronted Ben about what he had done, but Ben argued that his project was truly useful, not just an act of theft. "Nothing is useful that is not honest," Josiah said. Ben knew Josiah was right, and it was a lesson about honesty Ben would never forget.

Josiah was known for being honest and fair. Leaders in the community often asked his opinion on important issues. He also helped settle private disputes by serving as an arbitrator when asked. With 17 children, Josiah likely had to use these same skills to settle arguments at home, too.

While Josiah didn't always side with him in arguments, Ben was Josiah's favorite child. Josiah realized Ben was fascinated by the big ships in the harbor and dreamed of sailing away from Boston to live on the high seas, as one of his older brothers had done. Josiah, however, had other ideas for Ben.

When Ben was just 8 years old, Josiah decided that Ben would become a minister. Josiah enrolled his son in the local grammar school, where Ben quickly went to the top of his class. Josiah soon realized, though, that he couldn't afford to send Ben to college to become a minister. He dropped his plans for educating Ben for the ministry and sent him to a school where he'd learn more about writing and math. 🐦

3 THE YOUNG APPRENTICE

❦

When Ben was 10, Josiah decided Ben should learn a useful trade. After just two years of formal education, Ben quit school and went off to work. Josiah decided Ben would serve as an apprentice in his candle-making shop. Serving as an apprentice was a common path for boys like Ben. They worked for master tradesmen for several years, and in the process they learned the skills that would help them make a living for the rest of their lives. Josiah hoped Ben would follow in his footsteps and one day take over the family business.

Ben filled candle molds, cut candlewicks, ran errands for his father, and watched the shop when needed. But Ben hated making candles. He found the work boring, and the long hours seemed endless

Young Ben Franklin learned the craft of printing by working as an apprentice in his brother James's print shop.

As a boy, Ben Franklin poured fat into molds in his father's candle shop.

to him. Worse yet, the job literally stunk. Candles were made from the fat of cows and sheep, and the smell of boiling animal fat filled the shop. Sometimes Josiah gave Ben some coins for working in the shop. Almost immediately, Ben would run off to buy reading materials. He read magazines, books, newspapers—whatever he could find. Staying up late at night, Ben read by candlelight. He shared a room with one of his older brothers, but his brother always fell asleep right away and wasn't bothered by the light.

Ben's family was so poor, he couldn't ask for new candles to read by. Instead, he collected stubs of old candles that neighbors threw out. He used these stubs to read by after the sun went down. The stubs burned out quickly, but Ben used one to light the next as he continued to read. When Ben's parents discovered he was reading until after midnight, they told him to make sure he was getting enough sleep, but they didn't discourage him from reading. His mother even tried to find bigger candles to give him whenever she could spare them.

While Ben enjoyed having the money to buy books, Josiah knew Ben was unhappy working at the candle shop. Josiah also was afraid that Ben would run off to sea rather than continue working at something he hated. So, Josiah came up with another plan.

This time, he decided, Ben would go to work for his half brother James. Ten years older than Ben, James Franklin already owned a successful printing business. Being a printer sounded better to Ben than being a candle maker. At least printers worked with the written word. At the age of 12, Ben became a printer's apprentice.

James and Ben drew up and

One of Ben's older brothers, Josiah, had run off to be a sailor, which strengthened his father's will to find Ben a trade that would keep him on land. Ben's brother would be lost at sea and never heard from again.

signed a contract. James would provide Ben with meals, clothes, and a place to live. In return, Ben would work for James for nine years. By then, Ben would turn 21 and be ready to go out on his own.

At first, Ben's duties were limited to sweeping, cleaning up the shop, and running errands. Soon he began to learn more about the printer's trade.

The printing process was slow and involved many steps. Each page of text needed to be inked by hand.

Printers like James produced everything from posters and newspapers to books using a process that would seem very slow and difficult today. To produce a line of text, Ben lined up small metal let-

ters in neat rows. When he had lined up enough letters to make a page of text, he placed the rows of letters in a wooden frame to hold them in place. Then he covered the letters in ink. Finally, he put a sheet of paper over the letters and pressed the paper into the ink. When he pulled the paper away, it was covered in lines of inky text.

Ben didn't mind borrowing books from others, but he liked owning books, too. While working for James, Ben lived part of the time as a vegetarian. By not eating meat, Ben was able to save about half his weekly allowance, which he then used to buy more books.

The process was slow, and printers had to put in long hours. It was hard work, too. Ben had to lift heavy sets of metal letters and use his muscle power to operate the printing press.

His job wasn't the only thing keeping Ben busy. Ben was determined to educate himself. His new job gave him access to a variety of books and newspapers, and Ben was eager to read them all. "Often I sat up in my room reading the greatest part of the night," he later remembered.

In 1721, James began publishing a newspaper called the *New England Courant*. Ben helped him print and deliver the papers, but he wanted to do more.

Some of James's friends wrote articles for the *Courant*. When they visited, Ben listened in on their conversations and dreamed of writing for the paper himself.

The first issue of the New England Courant came out on August 7, 1721. The Courant was the first American newspaper not owned and edited by a postmaster. In those days, postmasters could mail newspapers for free. They also could stop other newspapers from being delivered, if they so chose. Ben helped deliver his brother's newspaper to make sure it reached its subscribers.

To improve his writing skills, Ben tried to copy the best writers of the time. He even wrote several poems about current events, which his brother had printed and sold on the street.

Ben knew, however, that his older brother thought he wasn't old enough or educated enough to write for the *Courant*. So Ben secretly left his articles under the door of the print shop for James to find.

The articles were signed by a woman named Silence Dogood, but in fact Silence Dogood was really Ben Franklin. James liked Silence's articles so much that he printed them in the paper. James's friends started discussing Silence's work when they visited the print shop.

Encouraged, Ben continued to submit more and more articles. Neither James nor any of the paper's readers knew who Silence Dogood really was. When Ben finally told his brother he had been writing the articles, James was furious that his younger brother had tricked him. Ben later wrote that the hot-tempered James beat him for deceiving him.

As Ben grew older, he assumed more and more

responsibility in the shop. In June 1722, James published a fake letter to the editor in the *Courant* that he had written himself. He criticized town leaders for not seriously pursuing pirates who were causing trouble that season along the New England coast. James was no stranger to writing articles in his newspaper that made city officials angry, but when he was discovered to be the author of the letter, the Massachusetts General Court took action this time and threw him in jail. While James sat in jail for a month, Ben ran the newspaper for him.

Ben Franklin sold copies of his poem, "The Lighthouse Tragedy," on the street.

Once out of jail, James didn't stay out of trouble for long. By early 1723, he again was writing articles that made town leaders angry. To stop him, the General Court forbid James to print his newspaper unless town officials reviewed it before it was sold. Outraged, James came up with a plan. The order applied only to him, not to Ben. Why not publish the *Courant* under Ben's name?

Both James and Ben knew that no one would ever believe James would let an apprentice indentured to him run the *Courant*. But if Ben were a free man, no one could prove he wasn't running the newspaper. So, James agreed to sign Ben's original indenture, saying he was released from the contract. This would prove to the sheriff and other town officials that Ben was a free man. He really wasn't, though. James made Ben sign a second, secret agreement saying he remained indentured to James until he turned 21. Publicly Ben was free, but secretly he was not.

Ben agreed to the plan, though. This was his big chance to have more influence over what was printed in the *Courant*. In time, the newspaper started to take on more of Ben's wit and personality.

Ben loved the work, but hated working with James. The brothers continued to argue, and Ben sometimes suffered more beatings at his brother's hands. Eventually, Ben had enough.

The experience Ben gained at James's shop taught Ben he was ready to run his own business. However, he still owed James several more years of service as an apprentice. If Ben wanted his independence, he had only one choice. He would have to run away. ॐ

Ben and his brother James did not get along well.

Chapter 4
LIFE ON HIS OWN

❧⟨❧⟩❧

Ben Franklin was 17 years old when he decided to leave Boston. It was no easy decision. He still owed James nearly four more years of service as an apprentice. Running away from Boston meant breaking the law.

But Franklin was determined to go out on his own. He knew James would never say anything about the secret indenture agreement. If he did, James would have to admit he, not his brother, was really the publisher of the *Courant* and risk going to jail himself.

Though James wouldn't say anything about the secret agreement, Franklin knew James would tell other printers in Boston not to hire him. He would have to leave town to find another job.

When Benjamin Franklin arrived in Philadelphia, he was dirty, rumpled, and jobless.

Franklin's brother James remained angry with him for many years, but before James died, they made their peace. When visiting his family in Boston, Franklin went to see James. Very ill, James asked Franklin to care for his son when he died. Franklin agreed to make James's son his apprentice and teach him the printing business, which he did upon James's death. "Thus it was that I made my brother ample amends for the service I had deprived him of by leaving him so early," Franklin later wrote in his autobiography.

Franklin made his decision. Having little money, he sold his precious books. He then traveled more than 200 miles (320 kilometers) to New York City to find a job in a print shop. After three days, Franklin arrived in town only to discover there was no work to be found. New York printer William Bradford said he had all the help he needed at his print shop, but his son Andrew was looking for someone to help in his shop in Philadelphia, Pennsylvania.

With no other prospects, Franklin traveled the 100 miles to Philadelphia. The journey proved extremely difficult. The first part of the trip, he sailed in a small, old boat with the boat owner and one other passenger. Hit by a violent windstorm, the boat's old sails ripped like thin sheets of paper. As the boat rocked violently back and forth, the other passenger fell overboard. Franklin reacted quickly. He grabbed the man and pulled him back into the boat.

The group remained in danger, though, as winds continued to pummel the small vessel. As the wind dragged the boat closer and closer to the shore of Long Island and its rocky beach, the men threw out the anchor to keep the boat from crashing into the shore. They knew the rickety vessel would be destroyed if it hit the rough beach.

As the storm wailed on, Franklin and the two other men huddled together as protection against the cold, pounding waves and rain. Though the night seemed endless, morning eventually came, and the storm quieted. They had made it safely through the storm!

Franklin suffered on the boat for 30 hours without sleep, food, or water. When he reached New Jersey, he still had a 50-mile (80-kilometer) walk before reaching Philadelphia. On top of it all, he became ill with a high fever, so he found a place to stay. He drank lots of water and got a good night's sleep. The next morning he awoke refreshed, ready to start his walk to Philadelphia despite the continuing rain.

On October 6, 1723, after four days of travel, Franklin arrived in Philadelphia. He later admitted that he must have made "a most awkward, ridiculous appearance" on his first day. "I was dirty from my journey; my pockets were stuffed out with shirts and stockings, and I knew no soul nor where to look for lodging," Franklin wrote.

Having gone without bathing for days, Franklin walked down Market Street in his dirty clothes and looked for a place to stay. As he walked, he saw a boy with a loaf of bread. The boy gave him directions to the bakery. Franklin had very little money, and he asked the baker what he could get for three cents. The baker sold him three big, fluffy rolls. "I was surprised at the quantity, but took it, and, having no room in my pockets, walked off with a roll under each arm and eating the other," Franklin remembered later.

He also remembered a pretty girl who giggled at him as he walked past her on the street. Little did he know, she would later play an important part in his life.

Franklin may have appeared awkward and ridiculous on his first day in Philadelphia, but he soon started a new life there. Though Andrew Bradford already had hired an assistant, he suggested Franklin talk to Samuel Keimer. New to Philadelphia, Keimer was starting another print shop in town.

Keimer offered Franklin a job and found a place for him to live. He would stay with the Read family, friends of Keimer. Eighteen-year-old Deborah Read barely recognized Franklin once he was all cleaned up. She was the girl who giggled at his appearance on his first day in Philadelphia.

Eventually, Deborah and Ben fell in love. Franklin hoped to set up his own business and then get married. His opportunity came in 1724.

William Keith, the governor of Pennsylvania, was shown a letter Franklin had written to his brother-in-law. Keith was impressed with the young man. He visited Franklin at Keimer's shop and offered to set Franklin up with his own print shop. The governor suggested Franklin sail to England to pick out the equipment he would need to get his business started. Keith promised to send letters of credit along with Franklin

Governor Keith encouraged Franklin to go to England to get supplies for his new print shop.

so he could buy whatever he desired. Franklin jumped at the chance.

In Franklin's time, the trip from North America to England required a long and sometimes dangerous ocean crossing. Travelers could spend six weeks or longer on a cramped, uncomfortable ship before they reached their destination.

Ben Franklin hoped to marry Deborah Read after his return from England.

Franklin wanted to marry Deborah, but at only 18 years old, he felt they both were very young. Furthermore, Franklin felt he was still too poor to

take a wife. He also faced a long voyage, as well as time in England buying supplies. Franklin talked to Deborah's mother. He agreed with her that it would be best to wait to marry Deborah until he returned from England and was set up in his printing business.

Franklin left for England on the ship *London Hope* on November 2, 1724. The trip took nearly two months. Franklin passed the time by talking with other passengers and playing checkers and cards.

The ship pitched and rolled through storms on its long journey across the Atlantic Ocean. *London Hope* was strong, though, and held together. It finally arrived in London, England, on December 24.

Eager to get his equipment and be on his way back home, Franklin opened the letters of credit from Governor Keith. To his horror, Franklin discovered the bag Keith gave him was full of papers, but none were letters of credit. Thomas Denham, a Philadelphia merchant Franklin met on the trip to England, said he wasn't surprised. Keith had no money, Denham said. "He wished to please everybody, and having little to give, he gave expectations," Denham told Franklin.

Three thousand miles from home, Franklin found himself with no money and no way to get back home. He immediately began searching for a job and found one in a London print shop.

Franklin quickly impressed his boss. While most

printers used both hands to carry one large set of type, Franklin could carry two—one in each hand. At 18 years old, Franklin was nearly 6 feet tall with a strong, muscular frame. He didn't waste time, and

Franklin worked on this printing press when he lived in England.

he worked longer and harder than just about anyone else in the shop.

Franklin saved all the money he could, but after nearly two years, he still hadn't earned enough for the trip back to Philadelphia. In the fall of 1726, Thomas Denham offered to pay Franklin's way back to the colonies and to give him a job as a clerk in his Philadelphia store. Franklin gladly accepted the offer, promising himself to be frugal with his money until he had paid Denham back.

"I was grown tired of London, remember'd with great pleasure the happy months I had spent in Pennsylvania, and wish'd again to see it," Franklin later wrote. He had been in London for nearly two years, and he could hardly wait to get home. ❧

5 CITIZEN FRANKLIN OF PHILADELPHIA

Aboard the *Berkshire*, Franklin and Denham set sail for Pennsylvania on July 21, 1726. Franklin used the time on the ship to think about his life and what was important to him. He thought about the kind of person he wanted to become.

Arriving in Philadelphia on October 11, Ben discovered he couldn't just pick up his life where he had left it. Deborah had married someone else, but she was miserable. Deborah's husband had piled up a great amount of debt and then left her. There were also rumors that he had another wife.

Franklin blamed himself for Deborah's misfortunes. Had he married Deborah before he left, none of this would have happened to her. When in England, he had only bothered to write her one letter.

Benjamin Franklin founded the Philadelphia Union
Fire Company and the first insurance organization in
North America.

While Franklin was away in England, Deborah wrote him many letters.

Why would she wait for him? Franklin felt terrible. He vowed to be a better person. He would treat others better than he had been treated by Keith— better than Deborah had been treated by her husband. He would be honest, frugal, and hardworking.

Franklin also vowed to serve his community, outside of his workday. To achieve this goal, he formed Junto, a club in which people could share ideas and work to improve society. This type of club was popular in Europe, but only educated men were allowed to join. Junto, Franklin decided, would be limited to 12 members who had curiosity and wanted to improve themselves, educated or not.

The club met each Friday. Members talked about history, science, travel, politics, and morality. Each week, members would raise questions on these subjects for the group to discuss. They talked about laws—whether new ones were needed or old ones were working. In addition, every three months, each member wrote an essay on something he found interesting. These, too, were discussed by the group.

Franklin kept busy with work and Junto, but a battle with pleurisy slowed him down for some time. Six months after Franklin returned from England, both he and Thomas Denham fell ill and had to close the shop. Although Franklin slowly recovered, Denham died. Denham left Franklin a small amount of money in his will. The money was enough to let Ben recover at home without worrying. Denham's shop, however, never reopened.

Franklin was out of work again, but once his health returned, he quickly found another job. Samuel Keimer offered him a position teaching his apprentices. Franklin didn't realize Keimer was just using him to get his shop running properly. When the apprentices were trained, Keimer picked a fight with Franklin and then fired him. Franklin was so angry that he left the shop without taking his possessions.

Ben Franklin displays the printing press in his shop in Philadelphia.

Hugh Meredith, one of Franklin's friends from the shop, visited him later that evening to return the items he had left behind. Meredith told Franklin he thought he'd been treated unfairly. The son of a wealthy farmer, Meredith said he thought he could come up with the money to set up a new print shop if Franklin would be his business partner. Meredith's father would supply the money to get the shop going if Franklin would teach Meredith the printing trade. Franklin readily agreed.

Business was slow when the new shop opened in 1728, but they did get a small job right away, thanks to one of Franklin's Junto friends. As word spread about what good work the shop did, more business headed their way.

Franklin also wanted to start a newspaper, but there already were two in Philadelphia. Franklin didn't believe the town of 7,000 could support three newspapers. He soon got his chance to be a newsman, though. One of the city's newspapers, the *Pennsylvania Gazette*, was printed by Franklin's old boss, Samuel Keimer. Unable to write well or spend much time collecting news, Keimer decided to sell the newspaper in order to devote more time to his print shop. Keimer was willing to sell the newspaper cheap, just to get rid of it.

In Franklin's day, news was usually collected and printed by the newspaper publishers. Publishers didn't hire reporters as they do today.

Franklin and Meredith bought the paper from Keimer. Their first issue of the *Pennsylvania Gazette* hit the streets on October 2, 1729.

Franklin wanted the newspaper to be successful. He worked hard to fill it with news people needed to know. He also used his sense of humor and printed lively stories that would make people want to pick up each issue. He made sure his stories were accurate.

Under Ben Franklin's leadership, the Pennsylvania Gazette *became a very successful newspaper.*

Franklin also took pride in keeping the printing clean, sharp, and free from smears. The differences between the *Pennsylvania Gazette* and its competitor were clear for everyone to see. It didn't take long for community leaders to notice and pass on the word to others. In time, Franklin's print shop became the official printer for Pennsylvania,

Delaware, and New Jersey. Franklin printed documents, laws, treaties, and paper money for each of these colonies.

In addition to publishing the newspaper and running the printing business, Franklin and Meredith also sold paper, ink, and other goods. The business thrived, thanks in large part to the 12- to 15-hour days Franklin was working, which didn't go unnoticed.

"The industry of Franklin is superior to anything I ever saw of the kind," said Patrick Baird, a Philadelphia physician. Baird continued, "I see him still at work when I go home, and he is at work again before his neighbors are out of bed."

While Franklin seemed cut out for the printing business, Meredith found it wasn't what he wanted to do with his life. Franklin understood. In 1730, with the financial help of two of his friends from Junto, Franklin bought the business from Meredith, who decided he would be happier working on his father's farm.

Word also came that Deborah Read's husband had died, and Franklin was eager to have another chance to marry his "Debby." However, some complications remained. Sometime in 1729 or 1730, Franklin had fathered a son, William Temple Franklin. Franklin never married William's mother, and historians don't know her name. Franklin had chosen to raise his son on his own.

Nevertheless, on September 1, 1730, Franklin married Deborah Read. She proved to be a good match for Franklin. She worked in his shop and helped raise William. She treated William as if he were her own son.

It didn't take long for the little family to grow. A son, Francis, arrived in 1732. At the same time, Franklin's career was growing more and more successful. His *Pennsylvania Gazette* became the leading newspaper of Philadelphia. In time, Franklin published several newspapers in the colonies as well as in the islands of Jamaica and Antigua. Not all the newspapers made money, but that wasn't really important to Franklin. He was more interested in making sure people could have inexpensive reading material. He never forgot his younger days when he had to save his pennies to buy books and collect candle stubs to read by at night.

Franklin's business also published books on home medicine. The books were important because many people lived in remote areas of the colonies far from any doctors.

In 1732, Franklin also began publishing *Poor Richard's Almanack*, a witty collection of advice, humor, and useful facts. In addition, the almanac included predictions on the weather and other events that would happen in the coming year.

While other publishers printed almanacs as a way to fill time when business was slow, Franklin

BY DILIGENCE AND PERSEVERANCE THE MOUSE EAT THE CABLE IN TWO

DILIGENCE IS THE MOTHER OF GOOD LUCK, AND GOD GIVES ALL THINGS TO INDUSTRY

This illustration from Franklin's almanac shows that steady work eventually gets the job done.

knew an almanac could make money if it entertained its readers. He also knew most people didn't believe anyone could actually predict the future with much accuracy, so Ben vowed to make the predictions amusing.

Richard Saunders, or "Poor Richard," made the predictions each year. According to the introduction of the almanac, Poor Richard was writing an almanac because his wife threatened to burn all his books and scientific instruments if he didn't do something useful with them. Other publishers often used psychics to make predictions, but Richard Saunders made them himself. In fact,

> *Much of the success of Poor Richard's Almanack came from the fact that people loved the clever proverbs. Some of the proverbs printed in the almanac through the years included:*
>
> *He's a fool that makes his doctor his heir.*
>
> *Fish and visitors smell in three days.*
>
> *The worst wheel of a cart makes the most noise.*

Richard Saunders was actually Benjamin Franklin.

Franklin's strategy worked. People loved it! *Poor Richard's Almanack* became so successful that Franklin continued to publish a new almanac every year for 25 years. Each year, about 10,000 readers eagerly awaited its arrival.

As Franklin enjoyed more success, he took on a greater role in Philadelphia's public life. Because he loved reading so much, Franklin's first project was starting a subscription library in his community. Junto members often shared their books, but Franklin wanted to share the joy of reading with more than just his small group.

Under Franklin's plan for a larger library, subscribers would pay a fee to buy the library's first books and get it going. Subscribers would then pay yearly dues that would be used to buy more books. The library would be open once a week to subscribers. If a subscriber didn't return a book when it was due, he or she would pay double the value of the book as a fine.

In 1731 when Franklin launched his project, few people in Philadelphia were readers. Most didn't have money to spend on books. Franklin started the library with just 50 subscribers, but that number doubled within 11 years.

Franklin's Library Company of Philadelphia was the first of its kind in North America. Other communities copied the idea and started libraries of their own. Soon, reading became a popular pastime in the colonies. Franklin later wrote in his autobiography,

These libraries have improved the general conversation of

Franklin organized a subscription library in order to share his love of reading with his community.

> When trying to gain subscribers for the library, Franklin discovered it was best to be humble. People shied away from subscribing when they thought Franklin was setting up the library for his own glory. So he decided to take another approach. He told potential subscribers that his friends were organizing a library project and had asked him to collect donations from others who loved to read. Using this approach, Franklin had no problem finding subscribers to get the project started. He would use this tactic again and again, choosing to stay behind the scenes rather than take credit for his ideas.

the Americans, made the common tradesmen and farmers as intelligent as most gentlemen from other countries, and perhaps have contributed in some degree to the stand so generally made throughout the Colonies in defense of their privileges.

Most of his life, Franklin saved an hour or two each day to educate himself. He studied French, Latin, Spanish, and other languages. He read just about everything he could get his hands on. Franklin felt this daily studying helped make up for the education he didn't get as a child.

Because education remained a high priority for him, Franklin believed Philadelphia should start its own college. Students could then continue their studies in Philadelphia rather than having to go to other cities. In 1751, Franklin founded a school that became the University of Pennsylvania. He especially enjoyed seeing students take what they learned in college and use it to benefit others by going into public serv-

In addition to the Union Fire Company, Franklin organized a fire insurance company in Philadelphia.

ice. He felt public service ranked as one of the most important things a person could do.

In 1737, Franklin became deputy postmaster for Philadelphia. The year before, he had helped start Philadelphia's Union Fire Company. This group was formed because of an essay he wrote for a Junto meeting about ways people could avoid fires caused by accidents or carelessness. This essay was published in the newspaper and drew a great deal of attention.

People talked about Franklin's article and decided to form a firefighting group. About 30 people joined what became the Union Fire Company. Each member agreed to keep leather buckets and baskets handy. When a house fire blazed, members brought buckets of water to put out the blaze and baskets to save whatever household goods they could.

The group met once a month to discuss fires that had occurred and come up with better ideas for preventing and fighting them. As others in the community saw the effectiveness of the group, firefighting companies popped up across the community. Eventually, just about every man in Philadelphia who owned property joined a group.

Franklin's quest for safety didn't end with starting a fire department. In the 1740s, when England and France were fighting King George's War, Franklin helped

Franklin lived simply. He didn't wear flashy clothing or buy many fancy things. Because of his thrift, he was able to retire at a young age and still live comfortably. It surprised him to see how others spent their money. For instance, when Franklin visited one of his wealthy friends, he asked his friend why his home had such huge rooms. His friend replied that he could afford it. Franklin replied with a grin, "Why don't you buy a hat six times too big for your head? You can afford that, too."

organize a militia to defend Philadelphia against a possible French attack. In 1745, he also helped create a city police force.

Franklin was becoming a wealthy man. By 1745, he earned more than 2,000 pounds a year. In those days, an ordinary working man considered himself fortunate to earn about 15 pounds a year. By 1748, Franklin had gained enough wealth to retire from the printing business, even though he was just 42 years old. He reached a partnership agreement with David Hall, one of his trusted employees. The agreement left Franklin free for other activities while providing him an income. Hall would run the business for 20 years and pay Franklin half the profits. After that, Hall could call the business his own.

Many people thought it odd that Franklin would leave such a successful business. Had he stayed, he could have become one of the richest men in the colonies. Wealth, however, wasn't important to Franklin. He had better things to do with his time than make more money than he would ever spend.

"I would rather have it said, he lived usefully, than, he died rich," Franklin wrote to his mother. Franklin was not interested in spending his retirement in leisure. He planned to devote his time to science. ✑

6 MAN OF SCIENCE

ॐ

All his life Franklin had been curious about the way things worked. He often tinkered with things to make them work better. In the 1740s, he began working on a better way to heat rooms.

At the time, wood-burning fireplaces and stoves were the main source of heat in buildings. As Philadelphia grew, however, firewood became more scarce and more expensive. Franklin wanted to build a better fireplace—one that used less wood but still heated a room well. His solution was called the Franklin stove or the Philadelphia fireplace.

"My common room I know is made twice as warm as it used to be, with a quarter of the wood I formerly used," Franklin wrote about his invention. The Franklin stove worked so well that it became

In this painting by Benjamin West, Franklin draws electricity from the sky.

popular throughout the colonies. "The use of these fireplaces in very many houses both of this and the neighboring colonies has been, and is, a great saving of wood to the inhabitants," Franklin continued.

The Franklin stove is just one example of Benjamin Franklin's inventiveness. He invented many other things as well, including improvements to the printing press, a chair that could be converted into a ladder, and a new kind of candle. This candle, made of whale oil, produced a brighter light and lasted longer than ordinary candles.

Franklin also invented a musical instrument called the glass harmonica. This instrument looked like a piano, but instead of pressing keys, the musician would touch his or her fingers against a set of spinning crystal cups. The instrument became very popular, and composers such as Mozart and Beethoven wrote pieces for the glass harmonica. Like many early instruments, however, it is no longer very commonly used.

Another Franklin invention, however, can be seen today on the noses of people everywhere. Franklin invented bifocal eyeglasses. The lenses of these eyglasses were split in half, with each half ground to a different prescription. Franklin wrote, "I have only to move my Eyes up or down, as I want to see distinctly far or near."

Friends suggested that Franklin patent his inventions and get paid for them. He said he wanted

In this illustration, Franklin plays his glass harmonica by touching his fingers to rotating crystal glasses.

the world to benefit from his inventions, but he didn't need to profit from them. He wrote,

> *That, as we enjoy great advantages from the inventions of others, we should be glad of an opportunity to serve others by any invention of ours; and this we should do freely and generously.*

While Franklin chose to be generous with his creations, other people weren't so considerate. Without the protection of a patent, Franklin's inventions could be copied by others who could then get patents themselves. In one instance, a London man copied the Franklin stove and made a fortune.

Though they didn't make him money, Franklin's inventions did make him famous. But Franklin's experiments with electricity made him known around the world.

Franklin became interested in experimenting with electricity after hearing a lecture by Scottish scientist Dr. Archibald Spencer in Boston. He wrote his friend Peter Collinson, "I never was before engaged in any study that so totally engrossed my attention and my time as this has lately done." Collinson lived in London and was a member of Britain's Royal Society, the most important scientific group in Britain.

At this time, not much was known about electricity. Scientists had many theories about this strange force, but Franklin wanted to learn from his own observations. Soon Franklin had converted a room in his home into a workshop where he could test some of his own ideas about electricity. His son William and daughter Sarah, born in 1743, would often help or quietly watch. Franklin's wife looked at the room filled with jars, tools, and bits of metal, glass, and other items and just shook her head. She saw a cluttered mess, but Franklin saw something much more.

Franklin also used the world as his laboratory. He had observed lightning in the sky and noted its similarities to sparks of electricity. As a result of his work, Franklin invented the lightning rod, a device to protect buildings from damage by lightning strikes. Lightning rods soon appeared on buildings in Philadelphia and around the world.

Franklin used these models in his experiments with lightning rods.

In 1750, he published a book, *Experiments and Observations on Electricity,* in which he explained his ideas and suggested experiments. This book was translated into German, Italian, and French and brought Franklin great fame throughout Europe.

Yet Franklin still wanted to prove that lightning

In this famous experiment, his son William watches as Franklin shows that lightning is electricity.

was made up of electricity. One day in 1752, he sent up a kite into a stormy sky. Attached to the kite's string was a metal key. When storm clouds passed overhead, the electricity in the clouds made the loose threads on the kite string stand up. When Ben touched the key, he felt a jolt of electricity. Electricity had followed the kite string and passed from the key to his finger. The experiment was very dangerous, but it demonstrated the clouds that produce lightning contain electricity.

Franklin enjoyed entertaining his friends with electrical tricks. One of his favorites involved taking a piece of wire with many "legs," running an electrical current through it, and making it walk like a spider.

This kite experiment was just one of many attempts Franklin made to better understand this strange force. He became known as a pioneer in the new scientific field of electricity. His scientific interests, however, were varied. In 1736, when his 4-year-old son Francis died of smallpox, Franklin began to study diseases. He learned about the spread of disease and studied the new, experimental practice of inoculation. He also studied sunspots, magnets, and the communication of ants. He helped farmers by showing them that acidic soil can be improved by adding a substance called lime. He was the first to study the Gulf Stream, the current that runs through the Atlantic Ocean.

The creativity that made Franklin so successful as a scientist and inventor helped him in other ways as well. Once, when traveling, he stopped at a tavern. All he wanted to do was warm himself in front of the fire, but he quickly discovered that many others had the same idea. How could he get close enough to the fire to warm up? Franklin asked the tavern owner's son to take a quart of oysters out to his horse. Curious about the oyster-eating horse, the other people in the tavern followed the boy outside. When the horse refused to touch the oysters, everyone went back inside. They found Franklin sitting comfortably in front of the fire.

In 1753, both Harvard and Yale colleges honored Franklin for his scientific achievements. Later that year, Britain's Royal Society awarded him its highest honor, the Copley Gold Medal, for his work as a scientist. In 1756, the College of William and Mary granted him an honorary degree, and in 1772, he was elected to the French Academy of Sciences.

Although Franklin had just two years of formal schooling, he received so many awards and honorary degrees that people began to call him Dr. Franklin.

Despite his many inventions, discoveries, and honors, Franklin wanted to learn more. He knew even greater inventions were to come, and he wished he could see into the future. In 1780, he wrote to a friend,

The rapid progress true Science now makes occasions my regretting sometimes that I was born too soon. It is impossible to imagine the Heights to which may be carried, in a thousand years, the Power of Man over

The Copley Gold Medal, awarded by Britain's Royal Society, is similar to today's Nobel Prize.

Matter. We may perhaps learn to deprive large Masses of their Gravity, and give them absolute Levity, for the sake of very easy transport. Agriculture may diminish its Labour and double its Produce; all Diseases may, by sure means, be prevented or cured, not even excepting that of Old Age, and our Lives lengthened at pleasure.

Even in his old age, Franklin continued to discover and invent. In his later years, he invented a device to grab items from high places, a chair with a built-in fan, and a tool that copied his letters as he was writing them.

Chapter 7 POLITICS

⤞❧⤝

As Franklin's fame as a scientist grew, he also became active in politics. He was elected to the Philadelphia Common Council in 1748, his first elected public office. In 1753, he was named deputy postmaster for Britain's North American colonies, and he worked to make mail delivery faster and more reliable.

With the start of the French and Indian War in 1754, England and France were once again at odds. Franklin played a leading role in defending Pennsylvania against attacks by France's Native American allies. He was elected a colonel in the Pennsylvania militia, and he helped plan a series of new forts in western Pennsylvania. He also was instrumental in arranging for supplies for British troops who used Pennsylvania as their base.

Benjamin Franklin was active in Pennsylvania political life, as well as that of the colonies. He wrote many papers and made numerous proposals on behalf of his emerging nation.

Franklin urged the colonies to unite to help defend one another. He represented Pennsylvania at a meeting of seven British colonies held at Albany, New York. At the meeting, Franklin proposed a plan for the colonies to unite and be governed by a president and a grand council. His plan, however, was rejected. The individual colonies were not ready to give up power to a new central government.

In 1757, the Pennsylvania assembly appointed Franklin to serve as its representative in England. He would have to move to London. "In two years at farthest I hope to settle all my affairs in such a manner, as that I may then conveniently remove to England, provided we can persuade the good woman to cross the seas," Franklin wrote in a letter to an English friend.

Franklin took his son, William, with him to England in 1757. They traveled throughout Europe, including Scotland, Belgium, and Holland. They also visited relatives in Ecton, England, where Franklin's father had lived before moving to the colonies in 1683.

The "good woman" Franklin wrote about was his wife, Deborah, who was terrified of ships and water. Fearing a long and hazardous sea journey, she wouldn't consider moving. As it turned out, Franklin and Deborah spent most of the rest of their married life apart from each other. He remained in England for much of the next two decades.

While Franklin was away, relations between Great Britain and its American colonies grew strained. Great Britain had gained vast new territories in North America through its war with France. The war, however, also drained British funds. To pay for the war effort, the British government introduced new taxes on its American colonies. Those taxes were met with howls of protest from American colonists who claimed that Parliament had no right to tax them without their approval.

One set of taxes, known as the Stamp Act, particularly angered colonists. The Stamp Act taxed marriage licenses, newspapers, wills, and other

Colonists protested the new taxes of the Stamp Act by burning royal stamps in a bonfire.

common documents. Each document was required to carry a royal stamp, which the government sold.

Franklin warned Britain's lawmakers that the Stamp Act would anger the colonists, but they ignored him. Yet Britain couldn't ignore the riots that broke out in New York City and Boston as a result of these new taxes. Franklin spent nearly every moment of his day talking to British lawmakers and getting letters from the colonies about the Stamp Act printed in British newspapers. The colonists even signed agreements not to buy products from England until the Stamp Act was repealed.

On February 13, 1766, Franklin appeared before Parliament and gave a heartfelt speech. He detailed the taxes the colonists already paid and refuted claims that all colonists were rich. He explained that colonists living in remote areas couldn't get married or write wills because they had to travel so far and pay so much money to get a royal stamp.

His speech also carried a warning. The colonies' population continued to grow. With 300,000 able-bodied men already living in the colonies, a rather impressive army could be formed if they chose to fight. Even if things didn't go that far, the colonies could hurt Great Britain economically by refusing to purchase its goods.

Franklin ended his speech by saying the consequences of not repealing the Stamp Act could be costly to Britain. The result could be "a total loss of the respect and affection the people of America bear this country, and of all the commerce that depends on that respect and affection," he said.

The following week, the Stamp Act was repealed. Newspapers in nearly every colony printed Franklin's speech. His popularity soared in the colonies.

The British government soon imposed new taxes on the colonists, however, and this time Franklin could not stop them. The new taxes prompted new protests in Boston and other colonial cities. In 1773, a Boston mob protested the new tax on tea by destroying thousands of pounds of tea

Franklin appeared before Britain's Parliament to argue against the Stamp Act.

waiting to be unloaded from a ship in Boston Harbor. The event later came to be called the Boston Tea Party, and it alarmed the British government in London. The protests grew into riots. The British government looked for someone to blame for the disorder in the colonies. They settled on the most prominent American in England: Benjamin Franklin.

British leaders accused Franklin of encouraging the disorderly protest. Members of the British government gave him a humiliating public scolding. To punish him for his support of the patriots, the government also dismissed Franklin from his job as deputy postmaster. Clearly he would no longer be a useful agent in England. It was time for him to return to Philadelphia.

Sadly, his return came too late for Deborah Franklin. She had continued to live in Philadelphia during her husband's long stay in England. She died in 1774 after a long illness.

Franklin returned home to Philadelphia in March of the fol-

> *For as long as he possibly could, Franklin held on to the hope that war could be avoided between Great Britain and the American colonies. During his last day in London, he sorted through bundles of newspapers that had come from the colonies. He pointed out articles he thought might help the colonists' cause if reprinted in British papers. An English friend who helped Franklin go through the papers later remembered that day and Franklin's sadness: "He was frequently not able to proceed for the tears literally running down his cheeks."*

lowing year. His sea voyage to Philadelphia took more than six weeks. While Franklin was at sea, the clashes between Britain and the American colonies intensified until, on April 19, 1775, in Lexington, Massachusetts, a British officer confronted 70 armed American Minutemen. When ordered to disperse, one American responded with a shot.

A battle later that day in the nearby town of Concord prompted American writer Ralph Waldo Emerson to compose a poem in which he referred to the Concord militia's collective musket fire as "the shot heard round the world." The American Revolution had begun. ❧

Deborah Franklin and her husband lived most of their married life on two different continents.

Chapter
8 A NEW NATION

❧❧❧

Almost as soon as his ship arrived in Philadelphia, Franklin went to work for the American cause. The day after he returned home, he was selected to represent Pennsylvania in the Second Continental Congress. Later, he was asked to serve as the president of the Committee of Safety, which was planning the defense of Pennsylvania. One of the problems facing the committee was a lack of weapons and ammunition. As usual, Franklin proposed an original and unique solution. He suggested the patriots use bows and arrows, but his suggestion was rejected.

Franklin also established a new post office for the colonies and helped George Washington organize the new army. Franklin's many duties kept him so busy that he wrote to a friend,

Benjamin Franklin helped Thomas Jefferson write the Declaration of Independence..

My time was never more fully employed. In the morning at 6, I am at the committee of safety, appointed by the assembly to put the province in a state of defense; which committee holds till near 9, when I am at the congress, and that sits till after 4 in the afternoon.

Franklin's work in the American Revolution led him to leave behind old friends and even family members who remained loyal to Great Britain. He cut off contact with his son William after his son chose to side with Great Britain. Not long after Franklin returned to Philadelphia, he wrote a letter to an old British friend named William Strahan:

Some of Franklin's political enemies accused him of being a spy during the American Revolution. As proof, they pointed to the fact that he had spent a great deal of time in England and that his son William remained loyal to the British. Of course, the accusations were false.

Mr. Strahan, You are a member of Parliament, and one of that majority which has doomed my country to destruction. ... Look upon your hands! They are stained with the blood of your relations! You and I were long friends. You are now my enemy and I am yours, B. Franklin.

For years, Franklin had worked to preserve peace between Britain and the colonies. Once the war

American victory
British victory

Quebec, 1775

CANADA

Lake Superior

Montreal

Mass.

St. Lawrence River

Lake Huron

Lake Michigan

Fort Ticonderoga, 1777

Lake Ontario

Fort Ticonderoga, 1775
N.H.

Concord, 1775

Bunker Hill, 1775

Saratoga, 1777

Albany • Lexington, Boston
1775

Mass.

Lake Erie

N.Y. Conn.

Newport, 1778

R.I.

Pa.
Trenton, 1776

Battle of Long Island, 1776

Germantown, 1777

Princeton, 1777

Valley Forge •

N.J.

Ohio River

Md. Del.

Brandywine Creek, 1777

BRITISH
NORTH AMERICA

Appalachian Mountains

Virginia

Richmond •

Yorktown, 1781

Atlantic
Ocean

Guilford Courthouse,
1781

N.C.

Kings Mountain,
1780

Cowpens, 1781

Camden, 1780

• Wilmington

S.C.

Mississippi River

Georgia

Charleston,
1780

Proclamation Line
of 1763

Savannah,
1778

N
W   E
S

West
Florida

0   200 miles

0   200 kilometers

East
Florida

began, he put aside his old loyalties to Britain. He and Thomas Jefferson, a delegate from Virginia, became two of the strongest voices for American

Major battles of the American Revolution were fought throughout the colonies.

independence. As a member of the Continental Congress, Franklin helped put forward a plan for uniting the colonies as an independent nation. Not everyone in Congress was ready to take that step, however. The war continued for more than a year before Congress finally began considering independence.

In June 1776, Richard Henry Lee of Virginia introduced a resolution for Congress to debate and vote on. It declared that the colonies "are and of right ought to be free and independent states." Congress formed a committee of five members to write a statement explaining to the world why the colonies should be independent. Franklin was selected for the committee, along with Thomas Jefferson, John Adams, Roger Sherman, and Robert Livingston. Jefferson wrote the document, with Franklin and the others helping him by editing his work. On July 4, 1776, Congress voted to accept the Declaration of Independence. Franklin and the other members of Congress signed the document about one month later.

After John Hancock, president of the Congress, signed the declaration, he said, "We must be unanimous, there must be no pulling different ways; we must all hang together." They knew that in the eyes of the British government they were now traitors and could pay with their lives. As often happened, Franklin broke the tension of the

This draft of the Declaration of Independence shows edits made by Franklin and others.

moment with his wit. "Yes," he said, "we must indeed all hang together, or most assuredly we shall all hang separately."

Of course, the Declaration of Independence

would mean little if the new United States could not defeat the mighty British army and navy. To do that, the new nation needed help. Because France had long been a rival of Great Britain, the United States turned to France for money and military support.

Congress chose Franklin to help negotiate an alliance with France. Along with Silas Deane and Arthur Lee, he would go to France to convince the French government to help the United States win its independence. Franklin was now 70 years old, and he faced another difficult sea journey to Europe. This time, there would be the added danger of attack by British warships. "I am old and good for nothing," he complained to a friend. But his new nation needed him.

As it turned out, Franklin played an important role in winning French support. His fame as a scientist, inventor, and diplomat had spread to France. To the French people, he was the most famous of all Americans. In fact, they saw him as a symbol of the new United States.

Franklin settled in the small town of Passy, just outside Paris.

Franklin took two of his grandsons with him to France: Temple Franklin, William's son, and Benjamin "Benny" Bache, Sarah's son. Instead of supporting Great Britain like his father did, Temple was on the side of his grandfather when the Revolutionary War broke out. In France, Temple assisted his aging grandfather and helped care for Benny, who turned 7 before the trio left for France.

In his plain clothes, glasses, and fur hat, Franklin was easy to recognize on the streets of Paris. Compared to French diplomats and royalty, Franklin's manner and dress were a refreshing change of pace. He was such a popular figure that paintings and images of him sold quickly in France. Even dolls were created to resemble him. Women created a new hairstyle based on Franklin's fur hat. They called it *Coiffure à la Franklin*.

Franklin used this goodwill to secure French support for the American Revolution. The French were uncertain if it was wise to form an alliance

Benjamin Franklin was a frequent and popular visitor to the French court.

with the American colonies, since doing so would mean war with Britain. Nevertheless, with patience and skillful diplomacy, Franklin convinced France to enter into a formal alliance with the United States. France publicly announced the alliance on March 20, 1778. Now, along with sending weapons and ammunition, France would send an army and a fleet of warships to fight alongside the Americans against Great Britain.

France's support was vital to the success of the American Revolution. In 1781, French troops helped George Washington's Continental Army trap the British army at Yorktown, Virginia. Surrounded by Washington and his French allies, the British surrendered on October 16, 1781. The United States had won its independence.

Now an old man and still living in France, Franklin had asked Congress three times in five years to release him from his overseas duty. In March 1781, Franklin wrote:

I have passed my seventy-fifth year, and I find that the long and severe fit of the gout which I had the last winter has shaken me exceedingly, and I am yet far from having recovered the bodily strength I before enjoyed. And as I can not at present undergo the fatigues of a sea voyage (the last having been too much for me) and

would not again expose myself to the haz-
ard of capture and imprisonment in this
time of war, I purpose to remain here at
least 'till the peace; perhaps may be for the
remainder of my life; and if any knowledge or experience I have acquired here
may be thought of use to my successor, I
shall freely communicate it, and assist
him with any influence I may be sup-
posed to have, or counsel that may be
desired of me.

*After the siege
of Yorktown,
the British
surrendered,
bringing an
end to the war.*

81

This painting by Benjamin West shows the men who represented the United States in the Treaty of Paris: from left, John Jay, John Adams, Benjamin Franklin, Henry Laurens, and Temple Franklin, the delegation's secretary. The British diplomats refused to pose, and so the painting was never finished.

However, with the war's end, Congress insisted Franklin continue his work. He represented the United States in negotiating a peace treaty with Great Britain. Franklin and other diplomats signed the treaty in Paris in 1783. In the treaty, Great Britain accepted that their former colonies were now free, sovereign, and independent. The treaty also established the borders of the new country.

"We are now friends with England and with all mankind," Franklin wrote to his friend Josiah Quincy.

He continued, "May we never see another war! For in my opinion there never was a good war or a bad peace."

Although while in France Franklin worked tirelessly for the American cause, he enjoyed a rich social life. He dined at fine restaurants and enjoyed playing chess with friends. He also enjoyed many flirtations. One woman, a French widow named Madame Helvétius, was a special favorite. He proposed marriage, but she refused him.

John Adams, one of the diplomats who signed the Treaty of Paris ending the Revolutionary War, would go on to become the second president of the new United States of America.

During his last two years in France, Franklin found more time to devote to science. In 1782, he watched with fascination as balloons were developed. The balloons were usually filled with heated air or hydrogen and could carry roosters, ducks, or sheep in baskets hanging below. Franklin saw many possibilities for the invention if the balloon's basket could carry people. He wrote to an English friend,

> *This discovery might possibly give a new turn to human affairs. Convincing sovereigns of the folly of wars may perhaps be one effect of it, since it will be impossible for the most potent of them to guard his dominions. Five thousand balloons, capable of raising two men each,*

could not cost more than five ships, and where is the prince who can afford to cover his country with troops for defense, so that ten thousand men descending from the clouds might not in many places do an infinite deal of mischief before a force could be brought together to defend them?

After seeing a demonstration of this new invention, an aquaintance asked Franklin, "What good is it?" Franklin responded, "What good is a newborn child?"

After Franklin's departure, Thomas Jefferson was appointed the new ambassador to France. When asked if he was Franklin's replacement, Jefferson responded that no one could replace him. Jefferson would later be elected the third president of the United States.

Despite his fascination with life in France, Franklin was ready to come home when his country allowed it. In 1785, the Continental Congress passed a resolution releasing Franklin from duty in France. Worried about Franklin's health, his friends urged him to live out the rest of his life in France rather than risk another ocean voyage. "I want to die in my own country," he said in reply.

Now 79 years old and weak from illness, Franklin embarked on his final ocean voyage. He left France on June 12, 1785, and nearly everyone in Passy turned out to bid him farewell.

When Benjamin Franklin arrived in Philadelphia

on September 14, 1785, he was carried down Market Street. As he passed, a joyous crowd cheered and church bells rang to honor him. Sixty-two years had passed since Benjamin Franklin had first walked down Market Street as a poor and homeless young man. Now he returned in triumph to the new nation he helped to create. ✍

When Franklin returned to Philadelphia from France, he was carried down the streets by an excited and grateful crowd.

9 THE FINAL YEARS

Chapter

In his diary, Franklin rejoiced at returning to his "dear Philadelphia." Best of all, he was reunited with his family. He lived with his daughter, Sarah, and spent time with his grandchildren. In their house, he built a new library to hold the thousands of books and scientific instruments he had collected over the years. He was happy to find his family in good health and circumstances.

Not all of Franklin's family was together in Philadelphia, though. His son William remained in England. The relationship between Franklin and William remained difficult after William sided with Britain in the American Revolution.

Troubles remained for the new United States as well. In 1781, the 13 states had united under the

This statue of Benjamin Franklin stands outside Boston's Old City Hall and is one of the sites on that city's famous Freedom Trail.

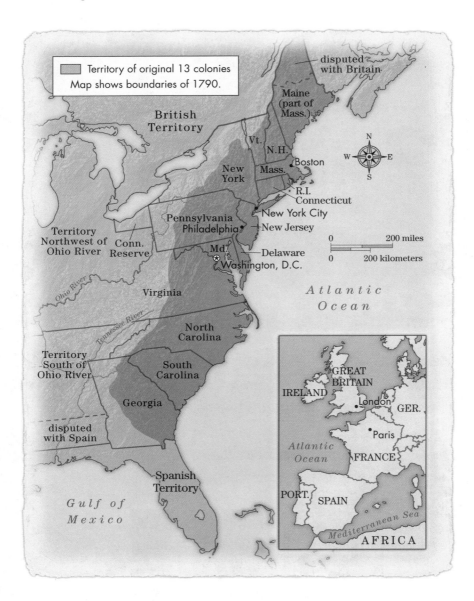

Territory of original 13 colonies
Map shows boundaries of 1790.

disputed with Britain

Maine (part of Mass.)

British Territory

Vt.

N.H.

New York

Mass.

Boston

R.I.

Connecticut

New York City

New Jersey

Pennsylvania
Philadelphia

Delaware

Md.

Washington, D.C.

Territory Northwest of Ohio River

Conn. Reserve

Ohio River

Virginia

Tennessee River

North Carolina

Territory South of Ohio River

South Carolina

Georgia

Atlantic Ocean

0   200 miles
0   200 kilometers

disputed with Spain

Spanish Territory

Gulf of Mexico

IRELAND

GREAT BRITAIN

London

GER.

Paris

FRANCE

Atlantic Ocean

PORT.

SPAIN

Mediterranean Sea

AFRICA

Although Franklin spent much of his adult life in Europe, he considered Philadelphia his home.

Articles of Confederation, but the union of states was a fragile one. The states argued about debts, borders, and other issues. The new Congress had little power to solve the problems facing the nation.

On May 2, 1787, a national convention opened to form a new plan of government. The Constitutional Convention met in Philadelphia, and Franklin served as one of Pennsylvania's delegates. At 82 years old, he was the oldest member of the convention. Five days a week, he walked nearly half a mile to the State House where the convention met. He never missed a session.

When arguments between delegates threatened to sink the convention, Franklin stepped forward. One of the big problems the delegates faced was how to settle differences between larger and smaller states. The smaller states wanted as many representatives in the new government as the larger states. Delegates from the larger states argued that this wouldn't be fair. Franklin proposed an important compromise that allowed the convention's work to continue. Franklin suggested that each state be equally represented in one house of Congress, today called the Senate. In the second house, today known as the House of Representatives,

When he returned to Philadelphia, Franklin added on to his house to make it more comfortable for Sarah and her family. Because they often entertained guests, he decided to add a dining room with a table that seated 24 people. The addition to his library made his personal space more orderly. At the time, Franklin had the largest private library in the entire United States.

states could be represented based on population. He helped push through the compromise, one of many made during the four-month convention.

With so many compromises, different pieces of the final Constitution pleased few of the delegates. Franklin knew getting the Constitution passed unanimously was vital. The new country had to stand united. Franklin passionately appealed to the delegates to set aside their differences, approve the Constitution unanimously, and present a united front when urging passage of the document in their states. Franklin told the delegates,

Benjamin Franklin and other members of the Constitutional Convention worked to create a plan for governing their new country.

I confess there are several parts of the Constitution which I do not at present approve; but, Sir, I am not sure I shall never approve them; for, having lived long, I have experienced many instances of being obliged, by better information or fuller consideration, to change opinions, even on important subjects, which I once thought right, but found to be otherwise. Thus I consent, Sir, to this Constitution, because I expect no better, and because I am not sure that it is not the best.

The U.S. Constitution was approved and signed by Franklin and the other members of the convention on September 17, 1787. After winning approval by the states, the Constitution took effect on March 4, 1789.

Meanwhile, Franklin retired from public life to work on his autobiography, which he had begun years earlier in an attempt to teach his son the lessons he had learned in his active lifetime. He continued to write letters and

After the Constitutional Convention, Franklin held one more office— the presidency of the Pennsylvania Society for Promoting the Abolition of Slavery, and the Relief of Free Negroes Unlawfully Held in Bondage. Although Franklin had owned several slaves many years earlier, he began speaking out against slavery as early as 1751. As president of the nation's first abolition society, Franklin penned letters to the governors of several Northern states and shamed them for letting merchants and shipping crews participate in the slave trade.

play cards with friends and family for as long as his health allowed. He wrote to an English friend,

> *The companions of my youth are indeed almost all departed, but I find an agreeable society among their children and grandchildren. Considering our well-furnished, plentiful market as the best of gardens, I am turning mine, in the midst of which my house stands, into grass plots and gravel walks, with trees and flowering shrubs. Cards we some-times play here, in long winter evenings.*

In January 1788, Franklin fell on the stone steps in his garden and injured his wrist and arm. Walking became increasingly difficult for him, and he suffered great pain from a kidney stone. He remained in bed for much of his final years of life.

On April 10, 1790, Franklin had another bout of pleurisy. He no longer had the strength to fight it. Benjamin Franklin died quietly at 11 P.M. on April 17, 1790, with his favorite grandsons, Temple and Benny, at his bedside. He was 84 years old.

He was buried next to his wife, Deborah, at Christ Church Cemetery in Philadelphia. More than 20,000 people attended his funeral. It was the largest crowd to gather in Philadelphia up to that time.

At age 22, Franklin had written what he then thought he wanted on his tombstone:

Benjamin Franklin is known as a founding father of the United States of America.

The Body of
B. Franklin,
Printer;
Like the Cover of an old Book,
Its contents torn out,
And script of its Lettering and Gilding,
Lies here, Food for Worms.
But the Work shall not be wholly lost,
For it will, as he believed, appear once more,
In a new & more perfect Edition,
Corrected and amended
By the Author.

In his final will, however, he chose a simpler statement for the headstone at his and Deborah's grave: "Benjamin and Deborah Franklin 1790."

In the United States, the House of Representatives passed a resolution mourning Franklin's death. So did the National Assembly of France, which remembered Franklin for his achievements as a diplomat and as a scientist.

And yet Franklin was so much more. As he wrote in *Poor Richard's Almanack* of 1738,

> *If you wou'd not be forgotten*
> *As soon as you are dead and rotten*
> *Either write things worth reading,*
> *Or do things worth the writing.*

Benjamin Franklin did both. His autobiography tells the story of a life well-lived. Franklin was a skilled printer and clever businessman. He was a brilliant scientist and inventor. He organized North America's first subscription library and created Philadelphia's police force and fire department. He was a skillful diplomat and a capable writer. But perhaps most impressive, Benjamin Franklin was the only man to have signed all four early documents most important to the United States of America: the Declaration of Independence, the treaty with France that helped his country win the Revolution, the

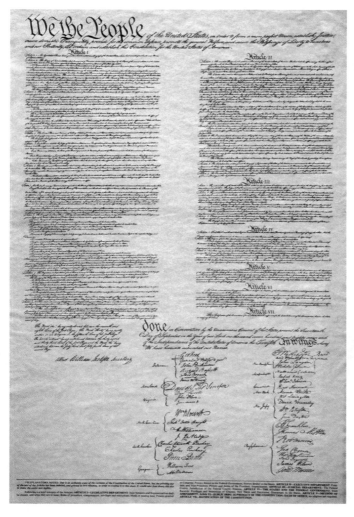

Benjamin Franklin signed his name to the four most important early documents of the United States of America, including the Constitution.

treaty with Britain that ended the war, and the U.S. Constitution.

Perhaps the French National Assembly summed it up best when it named Benjamin Franklin "the genius who freed America."

FRANKLIN'S LIFE

1718

Begins serving as apprentice to half brother James

1706

Born on January 17 in Boston

1705   **1715**

1719

French scientist Rene de Reaumur proposes using wood to make paper, which had previously been made from old cloth

1707

The Act of Union joins Scotland, England, and Wales into the United Kingdom of Great Britain

WORLD EVENTS

1723
Leaves Boston to begin new life in Philadelphia

1730
Marries Deborah Read

1730

1720
Japan lifts ban on Western literature, allowing new ideas to reach the island

1726
Jonathan Swift publishes *Gulliver's Travels*

FRANKLIN'S LIFE

1732

Publishes first
annual *Poor
Richard's Almanack*

1752

Conducts experiment
with kite to prove
that lightning is made
of electricity

1750

1749

German writer
Johann Wolfgang
von Goethe is born

1738

Englishman John
Wesley and his brother
Charles found the
Methodist church

WORLD EVENTS

1757

Moves to London to serve as representative of Pennsylvania Assembly in England

1775

Returns to Philadelphia and is elected to Second Continental Congress

1764

James Hargreaves creates the spinning jenny, a mechanical spinning wheel

1774

King Louis XV of France dies and his grandson, Louis XVI is crowned

FRANKLIN'S LIFE

1776

Signs Declaration
of Independence;
serves as American
commissioner
to France

1778

Negotiates alliance
with France to help
United States fight
Great Britain

1775

1776

Scottish economist
Adam Smith pub-
lishes *The Wealth
of Nations*, herald-
ing the beginning of
modern economics

1779

Jan Ingenhousz of the
Netherlands discovers
that plants release
oxygen when exposed
to sunlight

WORLD EVENTS

1782

Negotiates peace treaty with Great Britain to mark end of American Revolution

1790

Dies in Philadelphia on April 17

1788

The *Times* newspaper in London is founded

1783

The first manned hot air balloon flight is made in Paris, France, by the Montgolfier brothers

Life at a Glance

DATE OF BIRTH: January 17, 1706

BIRTHPLACE: Boston, Massachussetts

FATHER: Josiah Franklin

MOTHER: Abiah Folger Franklin

EDUCATION: Two years in Boston
grammar schools

SPOUSE: Deborah Read Franklin
(1708–1774)

DATE OF
MARRIAGE: September 1730

CHILDREN: William Temple Franklin
(1729 or 1730–1813)
Francis Folger Franklin
(1732–1736)
Sarah Franklin Bache
(1743–1808)

DATE OF DEATH: April 17, 1790

PLACE OF BURIAL: Philadelphia,
Pennsylvania

IN THE LIBRARY

Burke, Rick. *Benjamin Franklin*. Chicago: Heinemann Library, 2003.

Fleming, Candace. *Ben Franklin's Almanac: Being a True Account of the Good Gentleman's Life*. New York: Atheneum, 2003.

Gregson, Susan. *Benjamin Franklin*. Mankato, Minn.: Capstone Press, 2002.

Meltzer, Milton. *Benjamin Franklin: The New American*. New York: Franklin Watts, 1989.

Roop, Connie, and Peter Roop. *Benjamin Franklin*. New York: Scholastic Reference, 2001.

LOOK FOR MORE SIGNATURE LIVES BOOKS ABOUT THIS ERA:

Abigail Adams: *Courageous Patriot and First Lady*
ISBN 0-7565-0981-5

Samuel Adams: *Patriot and Statesman*
ISBN 0-7565-0823-1

Ethan Allen: *Green Mountain Rebel*
ISBN 0-7565-0824-X

Benedict Arnold: *From Patriot to Traitor*
ISBN 0-7565-0825-8

Alexander Hamilton: *Founding Father and Statesman*
ISBN 0-7565-0827-4

John Hancock: *Signer for Independence*
ISBN 0-7565-0828-2

John Paul Jones: *Father of the American Navy*
ISBN 0-7565-0829-0

Thomas Paine: Great *Writer of the Revolution*
ISBN 0-7565-0830-4

Mercy Otis Warren: *Author and Historian*
ISBN 0-7565-0982-3

Martha Washington: *First Lady of the United States*
ISBN 0-7565-0983-1

Phillis Wheatley: *Slave and Poet*
ISBN 0-7565-0984-X

On the Web

For more information on *Benjamin Franklin*, use FactHound to track down Web sites related to this book.

1. Go to *www.facthound.com*
2. Type in a search word related to this book or this book ID: 0756508266
3. Click on the *Fetch It* button.

FactHound will find the best Web sites for you.

Historic Sites

Benjamin Franklin National Memorial
222 N. 20th St.
Philadelphia, PA 19103
215/448-1200
Housed in the Franklin Institute Science Museum, the memorial includes a large marble statue of Franklin and an exhibit hall

Franklin Court on Market Street
Contact: Independence National Historic Park
143 S. Third St.
Philadelphia, PA 19106
215/965-2305
Site of a former Franklin home, now home to an underground museum focusing on Franklin's life and times

Glossary

abolition
the act of ending or stopping something

arbitrator
one who works to settle disagreements

Articles of Confederation
the 1781 agreement that created a federal government for the new United States of America

autobiography
the story of a person's life written by that person

Constitutional Convention
the group organized to write the U.S. Constitution, the document that states the country's basic laws

diplomats
people whose job is to handle relations between their country and other countries

indentured
working for another for an agreed-upon time period

inoculation
the injection of a substance into a person's body to protect against disease

militia
a loosely organized military group of people

Parliament
the part of the British government that makes laws

pleurisy
an inflammation of the membrane that lines the chest and covers the lungs

Second Continental Congress
a group of American colonists who established laws and addressed problems with the British

smallpox
a disease that causes chills, high fever, and pimples

105

Chapter 2

Page 14, line 11: H.W. Brands. *The First American: The Life and Times of Benjamin Franklin.* New York: Doubleday, 2000, pp. 15–16.

Page 17, line 4: Eulalie Osgood Grover. *Benjamin Franklin: The Story of Poor Richard.* New York: Dodd, Mead, 1953, p. 7.

Chapter 3

Page 23, line 20: Benjamin Franklin. *The Autobiography of Benjamin Franklin.* New York: Random House, 1944, p. 30.

Chapter 4

Page 30, sidebar: Ibid., p. 37.

Page 31, line 22: Ibid.

Page 32, line 5: Ibid.

Page 35, line 21: Thomas Fleming. *Benjamin Franklin.* New York: Four Winds Press, 1973, p. 22.

Page 37, line 11: Ibid., p. 25.

Chapter 5

Page 45, line 9: Ibid., p. 31.

Page 47, sidebar: Ibid., p. 39.

Page 49, line 11: *The Autobiography of Benjamin Franklin*, p. 107.

Page 52, sidebar: *Benjamin Franklin* (Fleming), p. 41.

Page 53, line 22: Edmund S. Morgan. *Benjamin Franklin.* New Haven, Conn.: Yale University Press, 2002, p. 29.

Chapter 6

Page 55, line 12: Irmengarde Eberle. *Benjamin Franklin, Man of Science.* New York: Franklin Watts, 1961, p. 94.

Page 56, line 24: *Benjamin Franklin* (Fleming), p. 41.

Page 57, line 3: *The Autobiography of Benjamin Franklin*, p. 185.

Page 58, line 14: Ibid., p. 184.

Page 62, line 24: Esmond Wright. *Franklin of Philadelphia.* Cambridge, Mass.: Belknap Press, 1986, p. 323.

Chapter 7

Page 66, line 11: *Benjamin Franklin* (Fleming), p. 75.

Page 69, line 1: Ibid., p. 84.

Page 70, sidebar: Ibid., p. 111.

Chapter 8

Page 74, line 1: *Benjamin Franklin* (Morgan), p. 220.

Page 74, line 15: Ibid., p. 228.

Page 76, line 9: Ibid., 231.

Page 76, line 23: *Benjamin Franklin* (Fleming), p. 129.

Page 77, line 1: Ibid., p. 129.

Page 78, line 14: *Benjamin Franklin* (Morgan), p. 222.

Page 80, line 21: *Franklin of Philadelphia*, p. 306.

Page 82, line 9: *The Autobiography of Benjamin Franklin*, p. 297.

Page 83, line 22: Eulalie Osgood Grover. *Benjamin Franklin: The Story of Poor Richard.* New York: Dodd, Mead, 1953, pp. 255–256.

Page 84, line 22: *Franklin of Philadelphia*, p. 312.

Page 84, line 21: *Benjamin Franklin* (Fleming), p. 152.

Chapter 9

Page 87, line 1: *The Autobiography of Benjamin Franklin*, p. 300.

Page 91, line 3: *Franklin of Philadelphia*, p. 343.

Page 92, line 3: Ibid., p. 346.

Page 93, line 1: Ibid.

Page 94, line 11: *Benjamin Franklin* (Fleming), p. 159.

Page 95, line 4: Ibid., p. 159.

Select Bibliography

Brands, H.W. *The First American: The Life and Times of Benjamin Franklin.* New York: Doubleday, 2000.

Cohen, I. Bernard. *Benjamin Franklin's Science.* Cambridge, Mass.: Harvard University Press, 1990.

Eberle, Irmengarde. *Benjamin Franklin, Man of Science.* New York: Franklin Watts, 1961.

Fleming, Thomas. *Benjamin Franklin.* New York: Four Winds Press, 1973.

Franklin, Benjamin. *The Autobiography of Benjamin Franklin.* New York: Random House, 1944.

Grover, Eulalie Osgood. *Benjamin Franklin: The Story of Poor Richard.* New York: Dodd, Mead, 1953.

Isaacson, Walter. *Benjamin Franklin: An American Life.* New York: Simon and Schuster, 2003.

Morgan, Edmund S. *Benjamin Franklin.* New Haven, Conn.: Yale University Press, 2002.

Wright, Esmond. *Franklin of Philadelphia.* Cambridge, Mass.: Belknap Press, 1986.

Brenda Haugen is the author and editor of many books, most of them for children. A graduate of the University of North Dakota in Grand Forks, Brenda lives in North Dakota with her family.

Andrew Santella is the author of a number of books for young readers. He also writes for magazines and newspapers, including *GQ* and the *New York Times Book Review*. He lives outside Chicago with his wife and son.

Image Credits

U.S. Capitol Historical Society/artist Howard Chandler Christy, detail of *The Signing of the Constitution*, cover (top), 4–5, 90; The Corcoran Gallery of Art/Corbis, cover (bottom), 2; Francis G. Mayer/Corbis, 8, 12; Library of Congress, 10, 49, 64, 69, 85, 93, 99 (top); North Wind Picture Archives, 15, 28, 33, 42, 63, 67; Lake County Museum/Corbis, 18, 25, 96 (top); Kean Collection/Getty Images, 20, 47; Bettmann/Corbis, 22, 57, 60, 72, 98 (top); The Granger Collection, New York, 27, 34, 40; MPI/Getty Images, 36; Courtesy, CIGNA Museum & Art Collection, 38; Stock Montage, 44; Lee Snider/Photo Images/Corbis, 51; Philadelphia Museum of Art/Corbis, 54; Erich Lessing/Art Resource, N.Y., 59; Archive Photos/Getty Images, 71, 97; Mary Evans Picture Library, 77; Réunion des Musées Nationaux/Art Resource, N.Y., 79, 100 (top); Giraudon/Art Resource, N.Y., 81; Courtesy, Winterthur Museum, 82, 101; Richard T. Nowitz/Corbis, 86; Photospin/Visions of America, 95; Hulton/Archive by Getty Images, 96 (bottom), 99 (bottom); Lombard Antiquarian Maps & Prints, 98 (bottom); Index Stock Imagery, 100 (bottom).

Out-of-work and Over-40

Out-of-Work and Over-40

Practical Advice for Surviving Unemployment and Finding a Job

STEPHEN LASER, PHD

To order additional copies of this book, contact:
Xlibris Corporation
1-888-795-4274
www.Xlibris.com
Orders@Xlibris.com
96796

CONTENTS

INTRODUCTION

By the end of 2010, the worst of the Great Recession appeared to be over. With that said, however, according to the *Wall Street Journal*, the economy still needed to add 100,000 jobs a month to keep pace with growth in the labor market. And at that current pace, the unemployment rate would not return to its pre-recession level of around five percent for almost 20 years! Moreover, with one job opening for every five job seekers, prospects for employment look grim.

Perhaps the most difficult part of the problem is not just the high unemployment rate, lingering north of 8.5 percent, but the fact that many people are either working in part-time jobs, unable to meet their basic expenses, or are underemployed in jobs that are not requisite with their education or previous training and work experience. These numbers are referred to from time to time as the *phantom unemployment rate*. Then there is of course the whole subset of people who are taking pay cuts and working fewer hours, and probably experiencing some kind of a reduction in their benefit packages, to include healthcare coverage and retirement funding. Finally, there are the truly discouraged former job-seekers who have stopped looking for work altogether and are simply not accounted for in the statistics published monthly by the U.S. Department of Labor.

The need for this book is obvious. With unemployment becoming a persistent, and perhaps intractable problem, the need to find ways to combat it are more compelling today than in any time in recent memory. My own journey to writing this book originates in volunteer work that I have been performing for the last ten years at various community centers, along with a number of religious organizations of a variety of denominations, all with their primary goal of assisting the unemployed at little or no charge to find productive jobs. Initially, I decided to become involved shortly after the dot.com bust in 2000 and 2001. At the time, a number of people had lost their jobs and were looking to become re-employed. By reaching out to organizations in the "business" of offering help, I felt that I could bring a different perspective to the job search process since I was neither a job coach nor a motivational speaker (believe me, I can sell *NoDoz* for $20 a packet when I start lecturing). Instead, *I sit on the other side of the desk,* helping employers evaluate candidates for hire.

Interestingly enough, even though the groups I spoke to initially in the aftermath of the dot.com bubble were substantial, their size would double and even triple or quadruple when the economy crashed, beginning in 2008. With some ebb and flow in numbers of participants over the past several years, the demand still remains for people who are desperately seeking help to restart their careers and gain meaningful employment. *It is toward the objective of helping these individuals put meaning and purpose back in their lives through productive jobs, that this book is dedicated.*

Whether certain people want to accept the notion or not, we are still very much a society in America which defines our identity by our work. Most individuals, when asked by a stranger to describe themselves, will typically begin by stating their profession or line of work, perhaps even their present (or past) employer, and then follow up with comments about their marital status or hobbies and interests like gardening, running, craft making, or NASCAR. Work consumes an enormous part of a person's day. Between the commute to and from the office to the time spent at home in the evening or on weekends reading emails and getting ready for upcoming meetings, the hours begin to add up, especially when the regular eight-hour workday is factored into the equation. With so much of our identity tied to our jobs—for better or worse—being unemployed is a devastating event and one that should not be minimized even by those who seek to define their lives with a broader sense of purpose.

In light of the trauma caused by being out of work, job seekers are gullible and desperate for any advice that will help them alleviate their suffering. Toward that end, there is no shortage of opinions, misinformation, nostrums, old wives' tales, and other assorted anecdotal advice in the career section (formerly the plain old want ads) of the Sunday supplement in most metropolitan newspapers. The advice givers are typically career coaches and life coaches who themselves are probably out of work and hanging out a shingle to generate income to meet their own living expenses. The result is a wealth of questionable or dubious advice. The following are examples of such winning suggestions: to include what to list on your resume; whether to use email or send handwritten notes; what clothing to wear for an interview, what not to wear for an interview; what body language to project; what day of the week is best to interview; how to hide your tattoos and body piercings (unless, of course, you are over 50), and so on and so forth . You get the picture. While there are a few useful nuggets contained in these (usually brief) articles, if you spend enough time reading these snippets, they will soon contradict what was said in an earlier advice column and further confuse you.

Most books that focus on the job search are written by gurus who spend their time coaching potential job applicants. Sometimes called "job coaches" and at other times referred to as "life coaches," these people, while well-intended in most cases, have had limited experience in the hiring game. Occasionally, a current or former human resources consultant or in-house HR executive will offer similar advice. These individuals are closer to the action on the front line, and hence, more likely to be credible than those who make it a profession of dispensing advice versus being a practitioner.

In my case, as noted above, I am not a career counselor or a life coach. The only coaching that I have ever done in my life was to coach both of my daughters' sports teams when they were in elementary school. In addition, I later spent time coaching underprivileged boys at a local YMCA after my children went on to high school. But all of this is grist for another book (or two or three).

In my day job, I advise organizations on hiring decisions based on the in-depth evaluations of a candidate's qualifications for a particular position. Our firm, which has my name, Stephen A. Laser Associates, uses a combination of testing tools and in-depth interviewing in order to make informed hiring recommendations. Therefore, I believe that sitting on the other side of the desk qualifies the author as able to provide a different perspective as opposed to the normal career coach. With over 30 years of experience in conducting pre-employment evaluations, there is a lot that I can bring to the table. Furthermore, over the course of that period of time, our firm has conducted as many as 1,200 evaluations in a single calendar year.

Malcolm Gladwell in his bestselling book, *Outliers: The Story of Success* (Little Brown and Company, 2008), talks about "the 10,000 hour rule." The rule is a simple one, according to Gladwell. Specifically, any person or group of people who have practiced their craft more than 10,000 hours are likely to be recognized experts in what they do. He cites Bill Gates and his countless hours of programming prior to founding Microsoft or the Beatles playing in a nightclub in Hamburg, Germany before their triumphal return to England. While I can neither sing (in the shower or anywhere else) and can barely navigate the latest technology (just ask the kids), I have well over 10,000 hours of evaluating people for different jobs. The information contained in this book is based on that wealth of experience in studying and participating in the hiring process.

Since the reader will be sitting on the other side of the desk from people like me, this book will not be about how to test or interview job candidates. Instead, it will present a *unique* glimpse into what employers are looking for when they make hiring decisions. This will include the actual behaviors and dimensions most employers consider along with a lot of proven, practical advice on preparing resumes, getting ready to take tests on-line as well as how to handle the tough interview questions that are typically posed to job candidates. Besides gaining confidence in your ability to handle test taking and interviewing, information will be provided on ways to make productive use of your time while looking for work. As many people have probably already heard: looking for work is a full-time job.

Another topic to be addressed relates to avoiding costly financial mistakes that drain precious resources which can ill-afford to be sacrificed when a person is out of work and looking for a new job. An entire cottage industry has grown, and unfortunately, prospered by preying on the unemployed. Various schemes from resume writing services to expensive, high-priced job coaching workshops, peddling unrealistic promises for successes or networking contacts, tempt the desperate to spend money they shouldn't be wasting. Finally, we have witnessed other examples of individuals who have received generous buyout agreements or lump sum payments of their hard-earned money from their company's retirement account and used those precious funds to go into business with a relative or friend, or even purchase an expensive and poorly researched franchise. In sum, we will help you watch your bank balance as well as navigate the choppy waters of finding re-employment.

Today's realities are sobering, and while this book will try to interject humor at various points (remember: it's all in the eye of the beholder), the purpose of the text will be to offer sound, practical advice that will work if you, the reader, take a disciplined and systematic approach to dealing with your state of unemployment. The likelihood of returning to the days of full employment along with plentiful jobs, as noted above, will probably be a long time coming. Besides straight-talk about the job search process, we promise to avoid buzzwords or business-speak. You will **not be hearing** terms like "thought-leader," "best practices," "visionary," "world class," "on-boarding," "deep dives," and other such trite, silly-sounding jargon and phraseology. Finally, as a licensed psychologist, I promise no psychobabble. In short, this book is written in plain English.

Furthermore, this book will **not** be politically correct in many ways. While inflammatory or derogatory statements have no place in any venue, social or business, the all-too-common habit of avoiding the "unpleasant truth" is often taken to the extremes. Thinly veiled references to the obvious are used to avoid important issues lurking just beneath the surface. In doing so, valuable information is disregarded in the name of pleasing the greatest number of people while offending the least amount. For example, who are we kidding when we don't acknowledge the obvious ageism that pervades the large layoffs in today's economy? Who's going to deny that if you are over 40, the job market is very difficult; for those over 50, it's almost impossible; and if you're over 60, your closest friends will suggest that you start to draw Social Security as soon as it is feasible?

Today's economy is no joke, and only through frank and candid feedback and advice can the unemployed in these age categories have any hope of finding re-employment. While I promise no guarantees with this book, there are ways where older and more mature workers can gain the advantage and use successful strategies that should prove effective in finding employment. At the same time there will be plenty of emphasis on avoiding the pitfalls and traps that can lead to false hope, or worse yet, part people from their money. Moreover, re-employment does not have to mean work that is demeaning or ill-suited to one's skills and talents as well as a person's previous education and training. At the same time, reconnecting in one's prior field is not always realistic, and in the long run, probably not always terribly smart.

To make this book a more readable and enjoyable experience, the author will not rely on humor, but; where relevant, stories and vignettes to illustrate or reinforce an important point will be included for the reader's amusement and edification. Over the course of 30 years in an employment-related field, I have enough stories to fill several volumes, but those that are most pertinent will be cited in this book.

The book itself is divided into roughly two parts. The first section of the book talks about handling the loss of a job, and more importantly, how to get ready for your job search. Included in this first section of the book is information on facing the new realities on job hunting in a recessionary economy, which is all part of an interconnected, global world. This means getting back into shape (literally and figuratively) to search for a job. The first part discusses making the most of your time while out of work by volunteering, looking for part-time work, and getting additional education and training as well as staying current where warranted. The first section concludes with valuable advice on how to avoid costly mistakes beyond falling prey to the many schemes and ruses that are on the market to part the unemployed from their needed financial resources.

The second part of the book addresses the job search process itself, beginning with a list of what employers are looking for when they hire an applicant. Interestingly enough, it is the identification and definition of these 10 to 12 attributes that was the original topic of the *pro bono* work I performed at various community and religiously-oriented locations catering to the unemployed. The second section, of course, provides very practical advice on writing effective resumes that get attention (without paying a resume writing service hundreds of already scarce dollars). There is also valuable information on doing your homework. In today's information age with access to the Internet, and search engines like Google, no job seeker should come to an interview unprepared or underprepared. In short, make technology your friend and ally, not your nemesis.

With 30 years of experience in the pre-employment testing and interviewing business, I include materials on testing and interviewing. The intent of this information, however, is **not** how to "game" the system, since nobody but the job candidate is being fooled. Instead, I address what tests are really intended to do and how to answer honestly and in your own best interests. With so many kinds of interviews in vogue today, information is presented on how to prepare for such overused fads as behavioral-based interviewing. Also, how to handle the tough questions in an interview are explained, especially the mother of all questions: "What are your biggest weaknesses?" The second part of this book concludes with a few brief but important pointers on your job references, along with tips for turning the tables in your job search so as to better understand the type of organization where you will be spending a considerable amount of time, should you be hired.

There is no one best way to read this book. Starting from beginning to end is how most people would approach it. On the other hand, if you are in the middle of a job search and about to take an on-line test or have an appointment for an upcoming interview, then jumping ahead would be appropriate. Moreover, if you are considering enrolling in a costly on-line degree program, you will want to focus on the information aimed specifically at that subject. Consequently, there are selected chapters on everything from avoiding ways to part with your money while feeling financially pinched, to writing a resume or gathering a list of references. In closing, this book promises to walk the reader step-by-step through the process of recovering from a job loss to making accurate assessments of whether your prospective employer will be a good fit for you and your unique talents and personality style. Above all else, I hope this book is helpful and brings hope to those of you who are feeling the devastating effects of unemployment. **Now, get to work!**

PART I

CHAPTER ONE

A Look at Your Job Prospects

People react differently to the news of being out of work. For some people, there is the obvious anger and sadness at losing a job, and if these individuals have been employed for many years, the intensity of that anger and disappointment is increased accordingly. For others, it is resignation after realizing that their organization, perhaps a failing enterprise over the years, is coming to the anticipated conclusion that all or at least a majority of the staff must soon be terminated. There are others who experience the feeling of relief that the inevitable has finally happened—that their insecure job has been one of several to be eliminated. Finally, for a few, there is even joy and excitement about getting on with their lives and finally being able to look for work in a field better suited to their talents and interests.

A Nation of Victims

For most people, however, the emotions associated with layoffs are neither pleasant nor reassuring. Simply put, they are angry and scared. The feelings of anger and resentment are obvious ones, but in addition, with so many people being let go nearing the end of their careers, there are the natural fears surrounding financial security. In the short term, people are worried about paying their bills and the typical financial obligations facing someone in middle age such as college tuition for their children, supporting aging parents, or being able to enjoy a lifestyle that many have earned after so many years of hard work. In the long term, a person wonders how he will be able to retire with any degree of comfort and economic security. With the rug seemingly pulled out from under them in a cruel and abrupt fashion, the unemployed can feel victimized and, occasionally, in their own worst interests, act in desperation.

Being a victim is very popular in our society. There are no shortages of psychologists and mental health professionals along with their friends in the plaintiff's bar who are willing to tell people they got a raw deal. In a day and age when people are less willing to assume responsibility for their actions, it is much easier to find somebody else to blame. The targets are endless: lousy management that had no business in the first place running a company; greedy bankers who overextended credit to companies that wanted to grow faster than prudently possible; Washington, D.C. and its needless and endless regulations that strangle any enterprise and prevent it from turning a profit; and let's not forget our friends in the Far East, the Chinese, the Indians, and other emerging economies that are producing goods and services at a far lower labor cost than what is possible in the United States.

Victimization is an all-encompassing ailment, and one does not have to be the victim of such macro forces as noted above. There are plenty of other excuses people can generate in their own defense. For example, some were victims of various forms of discrimination. Others were victimized by politics. Others so "threatened" their peers and bosses with their own self-professed competence that it became essential they be eliminated from the payroll. In sum, someone or some group of individuals "had it in" for the person, and now they are no longer employed. While not everyone who loses their job seeks to rationalize their job loss with such reasons, it is convenient, however, to assume that we had no or little role in the loss of a job.

To Sue or Not to Sue: That Is the Option

When people say they have been victimized, they often seek a remedy, and in many instances, it is a legal remedy. This is not to deny that there aren't appropriate times when people need to seek legal protection for being wronged. There are instances where people have been discriminated against because of their race or ethnic origin. As we will discuss in detail in this book, discrimination against an older employee is all too obvious. At the same time, taking (and wasting) the time to find a lawyer to sue your former employee is not necessarily in your best interests, and it can even be quite counterproductive. Later in the book we will talk about activities that drain unnecessary funds in your pursuit of employment, but in the case of filing a lawsuit, price might not be a factor. We are referring to the large number of employment suits that are undertaken by the plaintiff's bar on a contingency basis, where the filing attorney is entitled to a significant portion of the judgment should one be rendered against the offending organization.

Even if the price is right, filing a lawsuit against your former employer is not always advisable for several reasons. First, it wastes valuable time and energy. Preparing for a job search requires a lot of time and energy, and if a good portion of that energy is invested in finding an attorney and making your case against your former employer, it might not be the best use of your time and resources. Filing a lawsuit is more than just hiring or retaining an attorney. There are countless depositions to sit through and questions to answer as you prepare your case, not to mention the embarrassment of having your former employer present information that reflects badly on you and your prior work history either during depositions or in an open courtroom.

Second, filing a lawsuit against your former employer keeps you focused on the past as opposed to thinking about your future. The feelings of anger and revenge you harbor toward your former company will become an obsession as you think about getting your just desserts. Plaintiffs have been known to dream of hitting the jackpot—similar to winning the lottery—with a large settlement, when in fact, the price of resolving the case is likely to be much smaller than what you are anticipating or requesting. Moreover, a sizeable portion of the final settlement will be paid to your attorney, especially if that person has undertaken the case on contingency. Finally, in the end, no matter how the lawsuit is ultimately resolved, you will still be out of work and will need to look for a job.

Third, future employers might be wary of hiring you if they think they will be on the short end of litigation in the event that you are separated from their organization. Even though most companies will tell you it makes no difference to them if you have sued a past employer, it does make a difference. In a world seemingly gone mad with lawsuits for everything, few companies want to knowingly put a person on their payroll who has a history for bringing litigation against the organizations that have hired them. Even in instances where individuals were fully justified in seeking legal remedy against their former company, future employers are likely to discriminate against these people for fear of causing problems down the road.

In the end, you must decide for yourself if it is worth the time, effort, and extra energy to file a suit. From my perspective, lawsuits primarily advance the argument that you are a victim. This book is not about offering you a wealth of reasons why you have been victimized in today's economy even if you are an older employee who was eased out to reduce your organization's healthcare costs and make room for either a less expensive, younger employee or someone offshore in another low-cost country. Instead, this book is all about making you stronger and better prepared to take on the challenges of finding a job in a tough and competitive environment. In sum, you need to focus on the future and not obsess over the past.

It's All about the Three A's: Age, Appearance, and Attitude

Earlier, I mentioned that this book is not about being PC (politically correct), and in no place will this be more evident than in discussing the plight of an older unemployed worker who is also likely overweight to some extent and may become angry about their situation. While much mention will be made later in the book about the attributes employers are looking for when they hire people, hidden in this list are the three characteristics that often separate the successful job seeker from the person who is denied a job, especially during the early stages of a job search. If people think that age, appearance, and attitude don't really matter when evaluating an applicant's chances of success in being extended a job offer, they are only kidding themselves. In fact, personal appearance and the ability to communicate clearly and convincingly are probably the two factors that predict best as to whether a person will ultimately land a job, but more on that later.

First let's talk about age. There are a number of reasons companies discriminate against older workers—some of them based on pure business or financial reasons and others grounded in deeply held biases or prejudices. On the business and financial side of the argument, employers are often worried about paying people higher wages. Obviously, the longer the person has been in the workforce along with more education and years of prior experience and job knowledge, the higher that individual expects to be paid or compensated for his or her talents and expertise. Bringing on-board a significantly younger person lowers a company's labor costs. In addition, older workers are more likely to get sick and cost a company money in the face of fast-rising costs for healthcare insurance. On the other hand, there is the misconception, which is unsupported by hard data, that older employees will take more sick time and be absent from their job. In fact, the opposite has been proven to the case that the more mature employee is less likely to call off sick and abuse his or her personal time. Finally, the closer a person is to retirement age, the more likely it is that that individual will draw on a company's benefits and pension plan (if the organization is still offering one).

Besides economic considerations, there are prejudices about older employees and their ability to contribute to a fast-growing and changing enterprise. Many companies feel that in a day and age of increased reliance on technical skills, especially in the use of computers and other electronic devices, older workers are from another era—the Stone

Age. In certain instances, this is not an incorrect assumption as those who entered the workforce before PCs (which also means personal computers as well as political correctness) are behind the learning curve. However, as will be discussed in this chapter, acquiring computer skills and being savvy with the latest software and electronic tools is an important skill set to master in preparing to seek re-employment. There are ways to accomplish this without spending lots of scarce financial resources in educating oneself to assume these challenges.

Along with issues biasing employers against older applicants are the concerns surrounding personal appearance—another unmentionable, taboo topic in today's politically correct climate. Whether we approve or not, studies have shown there is a bias toward thinner applicants versus those who are overweight. Taller applicants will get a nod over shorter ones while attractiveness in general plays a much more significant part in the selection process than people care to think. Despite all of the statements that appearance is on the outside and it's what's on the inside that counts, the fact remains that personal appearance has a great deal to do with whether a person is hired or at least called back for a second round of interviews.

Does appearance matter? Well, it depends. For jobs where there is a high degree of contact with the public or a company's customer base it can be more of a factor than some would like to admit, especially when first impressions count in furthering a company's cause like getting a foot in the door for a sales rep. For jobs that would be classified as individual contributor roles, however, it probably is not very relevant at all. Unfortunately, job interviews involve making favorable first impressions, and hence, no matter how isolated the position being advertised, the ability of the applicant to impress his or her interviewer(s) is an important factor weighing on whether a person is extended an offer of employment.

Finally, there is the matter of attitude. Angry, resentful, and bitter job applicants do little to help their cause. Obviously, the angrier and more bitter and resentful the person, the easier it is to discern the individual's discontent. All too often, the interviewer or the HR representative at the company gets the full brunt of the applicant's anger. At the end of the meeting, the candidate might feel relieved and momentarily purged, but the poor company representative doesn't know what to think.

In other instances, a person's attitude is a reflection of his or her sense of defeatism over the whole job search process. There is no question that it is a grind. A hang-dog attitude that fails to inspire a sense of energy and optimism in the employment interviewer will likely lead to a self-fulfilling prophesy or another rejection letter, email, or voice message. It should come as no surprise that one of the leading causes of burnout with any activity results from trying so hard to succeed with little return for one's efforts. While there is no denying that constant rejection is one of the causes of burnout and depression, it is very important that the applicant find ways to keep his spirits up and maintain as positive an attitude as possible in the face of constant rejection, or worse, never hearing back from a prospective employer.

Counterproductive attitudes can also be apparent when an applicant makes it clear that the job being offered is far beneath the person's experience level and expertise. On other occasions, bad attitudes emerge when older workers find themselves being interviewed by people the same age as their children (or grandchildren), and their resentment is palpable. Remember, it is not the fault of the interviewer that he or she is younger. It obviously becomes a big red flag to a potential employer, however, if the job candidate cannot seem to get along with younger coworkers. The reality is that as we age, the workforce is going to be that much younger. Similarly, when older workers began their careers they noted how much older everybody looked to them. Clearly, it is easier said than done in terms of maintaining your cool and respecting the other person when the applicant draws an interviewer or HR rep who is arrogant or harbors obvious signs of ageism in his or her attitude toward the candidate.

Of course, age, appearance, and attitude are not all unrelated to each other. They do indeed interact in such a way that they feed one another. The older worker may or may not have made an effort to exercise on a regular basis or practice healthy eating habits. Moreover, the effects of aging and an appearance that hurts one's self-esteem adversely impact a person's attitude. Furthermore, extra weight or graying (or no) hair make a person feel older. Finally, feeling defeated and depressed can add years to our personal appearance and also lead to unhealthy behaviors like overeating, especially comfort foods like chocolate chip cookies and ice cream among others (two of my favorite comfort foods). In other instances, there are even unhealthier behaviors like the excessive use of alcohol or prescription drugs that can deteriorate our appearance and make us look older than our age.

While no sure-fire ways exist to eliminate all of the effects of aging, appearance, and attitude, there are proven techniques that can mitigate their impact. The key, of course, is to maintain the self-discipline to practice these techniques so that you feel better about your appearance and have a healthier and more productive attitude which in turn will lead you to be viewed as a more viable job candidate. In short, the onus is on you to show that you can contribute to an organization's survival and growth in a period of difficult economic times. Next, we will turn to a discussion of getting back into shape both physically and mentally in order to increase your attractiveness to a potential employer.

Getting Back into Shape

Getting back into shape means the obvious of physically improving your energy and stamina along with your appearance. It also means getting up to speed on new technologies and different approaches that are becoming the way of the world in today's economy. Also, as mentioned above, it means adjusting your attitude in order to compete for job openings in a way that shows you really want the job and are able to work with employees from diverse backgrounds, including coworkers significantly younger than you.

Getting into shape is also an important way of keeping score and meeting goals and objectives. In most cases, the job search is a long, drawn-out process with a lot more failures than successes. If a person is merely keeping score by the number of interviews he or she gets or the number of possible job offers made, success is likely to be few and far in between. Moreover, many of these goals are beyond your influence—they are in the control of other people. On the other hand, setting goals and objectives that you can manage and control will help build self-esteem and allow you to gain a greater feeling of mastery and control over your circumstances. For example, you might not be able to influence if a company will call you back for a second round of interviews, but you can certainly influence your ability to lose ten pounds within a reasonable length of time.

While we're at it, let's talk about weight. For many people, their sense of self-esteem is tied to their appearance or at least influenced in part by it. We sometimes wonder how we or someone we once knew got so heavy or overweight. But think about it for a moment: if between the ages of thirty and forty-five a person gains three pounds a year (an easy feat over just one Thanksgiving Day weekend), in fifteen years, that person can be 45 pounds overweight. Weight is an issue within your control, and between a healthy diet and regular exercise, you can go a long way toward improving your physical and mental health, especially in a time of high stress, which occurs during joblessness and unemployment.

The key to weight control as well as good physical and mental health is regular exercise. The range of options open to people for exercise varies widely. For example, an individual can walk for a period of time every day, perhaps from thirty to forty-five minutes, maybe an hour. Others can go running, and their distances can range from a mile or two to five, six, or more miles in a single outing. For certain people, going to a gym or health club provides a venue for regular exercise. These places offer exercise machines or indoor swimming pools, and some, if they are large enough, provide walking and running tracks. The cost of membership in a health club can vary from rather pricey to just a few dollars for a month's worth of exercise, especially if they are part of a local community center. The point is, regardless of your financial situation, there is really no excuse for not exercising. After all, walking or jogging is free with the exception of a pair of comfortable shoes.

A dirty little secret is that regular exercise could probably put a lot of therapists and mental health counselors out of business. Regular exercise has been shown to improve mental health and allow people to feel more positive about themselves as well as reduce feelings like depression. The accomplishment of specific exercise goals such as the number of workouts per week is helpful to one's self-esteem as is the noticeable improvements in one's appearance with the loss of pounds added over the years. As we stated above, appearance can drive attitude as well as the other way around. While there is value in seeking professional help as will be discussed later, one can make significant strides in improving his or her overall outlook and mental health through a disciplined program of regular exercise and proper diet.

Getting into shape is not just about literally shedding extra pounds, but it also means keeping your mind active and sharp. Again, like physical exercise, your options are varied. This might mean taking a class at a community college or at the local high school on a subject of interest or even one related to updating your job skills. Courses ranging from modern literature to learning how to use Outlook or Lotus Notes can all be valuable. As in the case of joining a health club, you do not have to choose to spend scarce financial resources on classes if money is a concern. Checking out books of interest in the public library or setting aside time each week to go to your local library to read periodicals or books of interest is just as helpful.

While watching the occasional television program or playing a videogame from time to time is not taboo, a steady diet of these two activities can be counterproductive as well as addictive, which in the end does little to help you achieve your ultimate goal of getting back to work. In fact, cutting your cable TV bill is probably a good idea for a whole lot of reasons, not the least of which is to save money and to allow you more time to interact with your family and friends as well as engage in the kinds of productive and useful activities just suggested.

The recipe for getting back into shape mentally and physically is to develop a regular routine and then stick with it. As will be discussed in more detail below, finding a job is a full-time job in and of itself. Having a routine is like having a job. It requires you to devote a certain number of hours each day or during the week to specific activities like exercising or attending a class in addition to pursuing your job search. To assist you with establishing a routine, let me suggest that you think about using a proven technique: goal setting. In doing so, goals should be measurable yet manageable. There is no sense in setting a series of goals and objectives you cannot possibly attain. Goals should also be specific as opposed to vague. For example, the goal of exercising four times a week for forty-five minutes a session is preferable to "I will try to get healthier and lose weight." While both are obviously admirable objectives, the former is more easily measured as opposed to the vaguer notion of improving one's health, regardless of how commendable and worthy it is to lose weight. Finally, for each endeavor—exercise, self-improvement, networking for job leads, or sending resumes and getting interviews—it is important to set a specific set of objectives and then track your progress accordingly.

The Decision to Seek Outside Help

One of the primary objectives of this book is to encourage self-reliance and allow you the reader to gain a sense of mastery and control over your life that you feel might have been denied to you by being terminated or severed from your place of employment. On the other hand, going through it alone can lead to chasing down blind alleys and increased anxiety and frustration at a point in your life when the last thing that you need is extra worry and stress. As a result, making the decision to call for help is a personal one, and only you, and perhaps your closest family and friends, are in a position to make that judgment. The range of outside resources is vast. Furthermore, the decision to pay for such help is an option, although many outside resources can be gained for free. If you do decide to seek a helping hand, I'd like to offer a few words of advice as well as outline the wide range of options available to you.

First, however, there are some critical issues to consider in making the decision to ask for help. For example, you must take into account what works best for you in terms of your learning style. Certain people do very well learning out of a book. They were good students in school, and learning at their own pace has worked well in the past and will very likely work well in the future. One of the underlying tenets of this book is that past performance is the strongest and most effective predictor of future performance. In light of this revelation, going to the self-help section of the nearest bookstore or similar shelves in the public library are recommended strategies or courses of action.

These same kinds of people tend to eschew group settings, where they are uncomfortable baring their feelings. They tend to be more introverted individuals who do not need to measure their progress or self-worth in contrast to a group of other individuals. For these people, talking in front of strangers is uncomfortable, and little is gained by their involvement in a group activity, regardless of how worthwhile the cause. This is not to say that taking a class or attending a job networking session is to be avoided. To the contrary, support groups in general can be very useful venues.

In other instances, however, individuals do well in group settings. They find the support they receive from their peers in similar circumstances reinforcing, and it motivates them to do their best. In particular, highly extroverted people do well in group settings, which tend to encourage social interaction. Additionally, competitive folks can perform well in a group setting as they identify a baseline against which they can measure their performance. For example, for individuals with these inclinations, Weight Watchers is beneficial as they seek to shed unwanted pounds. Support groups and networking groups also favor these types of people.

Another obvious consideration in the decision to seek outside help is the seriousness of the problem facing the individual. While meeting with a therapist or mental health professional might not be something you would normally consider or endorse for yourself as well as for others, it might be necessary. In the case of a person who is profoundly sad and moved to tears on a frequent basis at the thought of his or her former job situation, counseling of some kind is recommended. At the same time, if a person is prone to outbursts of temper and potentially violent actions like throwing things, or worse, hitting or striking people, again, outside help is demanded. Finally, a turn to non-productive or even destructive behavior like the excessive use of alcohol or drugs is another reason to seek outside assistance. Clearly, there are other examples of dysfunctional behavior that would warrant an outside intervention, but these are the main ones associated with periods of prolonged unemployment.

The choice of available resources can depend on a number of factors, but finances are a major source of consideration along with the confidence you place in the person providing the professional help and expertise. While those in the mental health field would like to think that their profession is a science, it is more of an art as much as anything else. It is true that while there are diagnostic testing tools grounded in statistics and certain types of psychologists along with psychiatrists who can prescribe medicine, no one mental health field, however, has a lock on curing people. More often than not, time or what is sometimes called spontaneous remission cures a number of distressed individuals.

At the same time, if you are suffering from depression or you are generally in pain over your life circumstances, getting some kind of help should not be questioned. Clearly, this book is not intended as a guide to the mental health profession, but the range of practitioners varies as do the fees they charge their patients and clients. Available to the individual are an array of psychiatrists, psychologists, and licensed social workers. The quality of help provided, unfortunately, cannot be determined by the type of degree and length of training the professional received in school and through internships and residencies. Finding the right person for you is a personal matter depending on your comfort level with the individual mental health care provider.

Not often listed as valuable help beyond the credentialed mental health professionals are those who are equally qualified to address emotional problems such as the clergy. Here, a trusted priest or minister or rabbi can offer help and guidance. Often, these individuals might be preferred in that they are familiar with an individual's personal circumstances, and hence, they are in a better position to offer advice on matters relating to the family dynamic. Finally, even a trusted friend can be pressed into service, but again, these individuals often lack the professional training required for the role. While these people do not charge for their services, money should not be the final determiner, especially if there is healthcare insurance to cover the cost of seeing a mental health professional.

Besides the value of counseling in terms of talking through issues and seeking support from those who have experienced circumstances similar to your own, it will be very important that you do not allow your anger and frustration to be directed at those who are considering you for a possible position opening at a prospective employer. In short, do not vent at your job interviewer. Unless your feelings have been addressed previously, your frustrations will likely surface during the course of a day of interviews and meetings with a potential employer. At that point in the game, all of your hard-earned efforts to obtain an appointment at the company will go for naught.

Accepting Today's (and Tomorrow's) New Reality

In this initial chapter on reviewing your prospects for employment and preparing for a potentially prolonged job search, it will be important to accept the new reality that is facing older candidates on the job market as well as those who are relatively new to the world of work: good jobs are going to be hard to find. When I began my career as an industrial psychologist in the seventies (that's not the 1870s as my children would have you believe), any prospective job applicant who changed companies every five or six years was simply categorized as a "job hopper." It was advised by more experienced colleagues in my field to avoid recommending these individuals to client companies. Today, that belief is a joke. Most people are lucky to remain with an organization for five or six years, given the high rate of mergers and acquisitions that lead to large-scale corporate reorganizations and job dismissals.

While the notion of a person having multiple careers—as many as ten in his or her lifetime—strikes me as extreme, long-term job security as practiced a generation ago is probably a thing of the past. Clearly, this situation is problematic since it means multiple job searches and accompanying periods of unemployment while these job searches are conducted. There are other costs involved, which include moving and relocation expenses along with the natural disruptions that are likely to occur as people transition from one employer to the next.

Added to these well-documented phenomena is the idea that the world is changing in profound ways, which will produce a subsequent impact on the world of work. For example, the world is now digital. Paper-based systems from calendar books to airline reservations are moving toward becoming electronic. In fact, an airline passenger pays a premium for having a paper ticket versus an e-ticket. While printers will produce hardcopies of electronic documents, the move to a digital world is here. Even more impactful is the Internet and the search engines that are available to people. As with everything, there is good and bad associated with these new tools, but the reality is that they are here to stay.

Hopefully, one of the new realities we're seeing as the twenty-first century dawns on us is not a steady decline of our country and its economy. Even though overseas competition has been around since the 1970s, beginning with the rise of Japan and Western Europe, we now are seeing emerging nations like China, India, and Brazil moving to the forefront to say nothing of resource-rich nations like Canada and Australia. Regardless, all of this change affects your job search either directly or indirectly. If your line of work is being outsourced overseas, that makes a difference. If you are functioning in an industry with colleagues all over the globe, your world is likely to be 24/7 in order to accommodate the work schedules of those people in far-reaching time zones. This means developing stamina and unique skills to deal with having to conduct a conference call at ten o'clock at night or very early in the morning around dawn.

In sum, change is all about us. The old-fashioned idea of a job for life is a thing of the past like leather football helmets and Model T cars. With smart phones and high-powered laptop computers and now iPads, the world is your office, and you are accessible anytime, any place. Get used to it.

Finding a Job Is a Full-Time Job

As this chapter indicates, there is a lot to consider before you write your resume (on your processor). Even before you organize your list of networking contacts, you need to address issues related to getting back into shape and preparing for a tough and competitive job market fraught with disappointments meant to discourage even the most daunting. In short, finding a job is full-time work. This means operating with a schedule and measurable goals and objectives, not unlike what you had at your job before it went away. You must make each day count and try to have something to show for your efforts. Persistence and positive thinking are, of course, difficult to sustain in the face of regular rejection, but you have the tools at your disposal to help you.

While managing your money will be critical to your emotional well-being, it is not out of the question to suggest ways to reward yourself for accomplishing certain objectives. It might mean a day off or a short trip to a museum or a ball game. You don't have to leave a mortgage payment at a professional sporting event. High school and local college games can be just as fun and exciting and a lot more economical. For some people, a reward might mean buying a DVD or a book. Even a trip to the mall if within your budget is a worthwhile reward for attaining a challenging goal or objective. Regardless, it is important to provide yourself with meaningful rewards in order to keep you motivated and on track.

Just as your former job was a grind on many occasions, so will be your job search. There are those individuals who hit it big and locate new employment within a very short period of time of losing their last job, but these people are few and far in between. Hard work, perseverance, and openness to feedback from friends and family as well as those involved in the same endeavor as you are all part of the answer to solving the riddle of finding a new job. If you assume that being unemployed is a new type of work (unfortunately without monetary rewards), you will place yourself in a better position. Remember, luck is nothing more than a meeting at the intersection of opportunity and preparation.

CHAPTER TWO

Making Your Time Productive

Vignette: One Stupid Guy And One Smart Lady

On a Sunday afternoon, during the height of the recent recession, I was forced to purchase a lightweight jacket to replace the brand new one my wife had gotten for me. The reason: I left my brand new jacket on a commuter train earlier in the week as I have managed to do with a number of my possessions, which include hats, gloves, umbrellas, and even a framed picture of my wife (don't any of you Freudian psychologists reading this book say a word). Returning home with my tail between my legs, my wife was forgiving enough to give me a couple of in-store coupons to purchase another coat at the same store she had originally found the one now lost due to my negligence. My wife also knows that I hate shopping, so having to go to the mall to find a replacement was torture enough. Thus, we have the part of the story about "one stupid guy."

As I made my way to the Men's Department, I was pleasantly surprised by the large selection of lightweight coats for my perusal. Unfortunately, as I made my way through the racks and racks of coats, all of them were either large or extra large in size. There were a handful of mediums, and no smalls, which is my ideal fit. Gifted with the patience of a saint, I fumed and sputtered my way to the counter, where a salesclerk was assisting another customer. In this case, the customer looked about as out of place as myself in a retail setting. The older gentleman too was armed with a few in-store coupons, and he had about $150 in merchandise at the register. The salesclerk was a bright and alert older Asian woman who quickly totaled the price of the clothing in her head and then proceeded to take off the discounts that he had requested. But then, she reached under the counter and took out a copy of the Sunday newspaper and showed him a few bargain pieces of clothing similar to what he had in his hands at significantly lower prices. She then made the appropriate substitutions of his initial purchases with the on-sale merchandise. If this was not enough, she opened a charge account in his name as opposed to the accounts in his wife's and daughter's names and gave him another 15 percent off the final sale price. Finally, for good measure she added a discount for shoppers over age 50 and brought his final bill to $34. My jaw dropped.

When my turn came to be helped my astonishment quickly gave way to another wave of anger and frustration as I berated the poor woman about the meager selection of lightweight jackets in my size or the size of any of the other members of the community who were equally as vertically challenged as me. After the salesclerk was good enough to remove the soapbox on which I launched by tirade, she said that many clothing manufacturers "inflated" men's sizes to make them feel better about themselves, especially if they were of smaller stature (imagine that!). She knew this because her own husband was my size, and she had been at the store several months ago and caught on to the system. Our energetic whirlwind then pulled no less than seven coats from the rack and she asked me to pick a color and then try on the ones that suited me best. When I had found the exact match as the one I forgot on the train, she substituted another one of similar style but about half the price. Then, when we reached the register, she used my wife's discount coupons to take another significant amount of money off the final sale. I now had a brand new replacement for just under $30.

As I watched this wizard at work, it dawned on me to ask her a rather personal question. Looking at her I said, "This isn't your 'real' job, is it?" Surprisingly, she was hardly offended, and she began to tell me her life story (in abbreviated form). The salesclerk explained that she was born in Singapore and spent most of her adult life in Japan working for an import/export bank before being sent to the United States to perform the same function she had been doing in Tokyo. During the recent downturn that hurt all of the major banks around the world, this thirty-year veteran of the banking industry also lost her job. At first, she sat around for a few weeks enjoying her severance pay. While she could have stayed out of the workforce longer when unemployment benefits were figured into the equation along with her husband's salary, she wanted to get back to work.

Rather than send out a bunch of resumes via email, she took a different approach. Realizing that the shopping mall where she was now working was frequented by a lot of wealthy people, many of whom worked in banking and financial services, she wanted to get direct exposure to this group of customers. She felt that if people observed her in action as had I and the others in the Men's Department that day, people would take notice of her (duh). As we drew our conversation to a close, she shared with me that she had already had five or six initial interviews, and she was looking at a few more, plus several second-round interviews, meanwhile progressing further with three of her initial contacts. In short, she would likely land a job within the next month. Hence, we have the other part of the story about "one smart lady."

Getting a Part-time Job

As in the case of our one smart lady, she was able to parlay her part-time position into opportunities to return to full-time work in her chosen profession. There are a number of reasons for finding part-time work during your job search. First, it adds a paycheck that can supplement severance payments and even one-half of your weekly unemployment benefits in some instances. Second, certain part-time jobs can offer health insurance. But beyond the monetary rewards for part-time work, these kinds of activities allow you to keep busy. A part-time job offers a place to go and an opportunity to socialize with coworkers as opposed to sitting at home. Finally, if you choose the right venue for a part-time position as did our former import/export banker, your opportunity for future contacts is greatly enhanced.

Many part-time jobs are advertised online or in the local newspaper. Also asking at places that hire part-time help is another viable approach. As in the case of the above-mentioned vignette, locating a place to perform part-time work can be just as important since it enhances your chances of meeting the right kinds of people. There is another side to the coin, however. If you are embarrassed about running into former friends and colleagues from work who might wonder what you are doing at the florist shop or behind the counter at a local restaurant, then be careful about putting yourself in a position that will cause you to feel awkward and uncomfortable about your new work situation.

In certain instances, you might want to get a part-time job in a line of work that is related to a hobby or interest. For example, if you are handy with do-it-yourself projects, finding employment in a home improvement center might be right for you. If you like to cook, working at a restaurant might be a good fit. If you are a fan of the arts, helping to usher at a local theater where you could also see the productions without charge might prove practical. The same goes for working at stadium venues if you are interested in sports. Several years ago I met an automobile enthusiast who went to work part-time at a local car dealership selling high-priced, high-performance sports cars that he had always admired. The part-time job soon gave way to a full-time position and a career that ultimately earned him as much annual income as he had received at his previous job writing software programs.

Performing Volunteer Work

The world of volunteer work offers endless opportunities for fulfillment as well as the chance to make invaluable contacts in a setting that is not as high pressure or as transaction-oriented as a networking party. One of the additional advantages of volunteering is the opportunity to showcase your skills in front of prospective employers and key contact people. For example, if you are skilled in finance or accounting, volunteering to be the treasurer of your community organization is a golden opportunity to let other members of the group observe your capabilities in action. If you are an architect or builder, you can either head or serve on the committee involved in constructing an addition to your church or temple. Finally, for those in human resources, taking the lead role in hiring a new executive director of your volunteer organization will provide a chance to demonstrate your knowledge of employee selection along with your talent in negotiating a compensation package for the person identified as the ideal candidate for the job.

Certainly, volunteer work, like a part-time job, keeps you active and out of the house while working in the presence of other people. Beyond simple networking opportunities, it is physically and emotionally healthy for you. Choosing the right setting for you is also important because you want to enjoy yourself and hopefully exhibit your talents and abilities while also performing a valuable service for your religious congregation or your community. In other instances, the proper choice of the right activity might allow you to try a second career option that allows you to do something that has always been in the back of your mind. Two ready examples are teaching and coaching youth sports. While your pay might not equal the level of your last job, the rewards and satisfaction might well outweigh the monetary aspects of your new situation. The chance to give back to others as well as help those in need while you yourself are in need is an emotionally healthy experience.

There is of course volunteer work that will involve keeping physically active while doing good for others, which can help you become fit and trim if that is one of your goals. For example, helping rehabilitate homes through groups like Habitat for Humanity or other community-sponsored organizations offers one extensive experience along these same lines. Many religious organizations take it upon themselves to assist with community outreach programs designed to restore and beautify rundown properties and neighborhoods. Obviously, if you are talented with your hands and have engaged in do-it-yourself projects around the house, these kinds of volunteer activities might be a perfect fit for you.

In closing, there are no end to the volunteer organizations that could use your help. Unfortunately, in a sour economy, the needs of these groups increase accordingly. But making the right selection for you is important. First, you should believe in the cause you are joining. Occasionally, individuals will join groups because of the networking opportunities only. This kind of purely self-serving behavior will be readily apparent to the other members of the group, and you will likely find yourself a pariah among your peers. Rewards and recognition from volunteer organizations will flow easiest when you join a group and embrace the members for who they are as people as opposed to how they can help your chances of finding reemployment. But again, if you find an organization that allows you to showcase your skills while making valuable contacts, along with enjoying the camaraderie of the other volunteers in the group, you will have made an ideal match that will not only probably benefit you in the long run, but also do good for a worthwhile cause.

Turning an Avocation into a Vocation

For every young boy who dreams of playing in a major league baseball game or joining the NBA (National Basketball Association), there are young girls who want to convert their thousands of hours of dancing lessons into a role on the Broadway stage or with a famous dance company touring the world. These are, of course, two obvious examples of a person taking a hobby or interest one step further and actually getting paid to do what he or she loves. There are other examples as well. Writers, photographers, painters, poets, and skilled artisans all fall under this heading. Losing your day job might offer you an opportunity to convert your talent into a paying profession. Certainly, the competition for these kinds of jobs is fierce, but if you have a special gift, this might afford you an opportunity to just go ahead and give it a try. Naturally, most professionals who teach these special skills advise aspiring individuals to perfect their skills in their spare time to see if there is an audience or market for a possible paying job. If you are suddenly laid off, however, you might just use your situation as an opportunity to convert your hobby into a true vocation.

No firm and fast rules exist for advising people on how to make this transition, but common sense offers some guidance. For example, if photography is your passion, you might think about offering your services for a small amount of remuneration or even volunteering them if there are no takers to handle the pictures at a special event like an anniversary party or a special family dinner. Taking on a wedding might be too ambitious, but certainly, shooting pictures at a prenuptial dinner might offer a chance to show your skills. Writing might present the same opportunity. You could offer to write a piece for a magazine on a topic that interests you like travel or dining out. With limited financial resources, taking extravagant vacations or indulging in fine dining might not be the best idea, but the publication requesting your work might offer you some financial assistance. Nevertheless, many local publications would welcome the expertise of someone submitting a story or two in order to fill their pages.

For the vast army of do-it-yourself people, there are ways to showcase your skills. During your unemployment, you might want to take on a project in your home or offer to perform work for a relative or a close friend who knows you and trusts you to do a good job. Allowing others to see the kind of work you perform, be it carpentry or plumbing or any kind of remodeling effort, gives you a way to demonstrate the skills you would bring to other projects. Starting slowly and building a small clientele where your reputation spreads by word of mouth could lead to real opportunities to turn that hobby of yours into a paying profession. Moreover, by concentrating your focus on small remodeling and rehabilitation work, you don't run the risk of competing directly with large builders and contractors who might find these jobs too small and not worth bidding on. Even if you do not intend to become a skilled tradesperson, just taking on a large home improvement project around your own house will allow you to work with your hands and see the fruits of your labor. Furthermore, the work will not only be satisfying, but it will also let you attack a project that might be too expensive to undertake by hiring an outside contractor, especially if finances are tight and the luxury of adding a room or converting an outdoor porch to an indoor one is out of your budget range.

Finally, there are those rare individuals who prepare for the possibility of periods of unemployment by taking steps ahead of time to hone their skills and get ready for the day when they might take those outside hobbies and interests and make a break for it. Many years ago, I encountered a gentleman who was laid off from his job as the CFO of a large manufacturing business. Our firm was contracted to evaluate him for a comparable position at one of our client organizations. He seemed like the ideal candidate; he was bright, urbane, gifted with excellent skills in analyzing financial data, and a genuinely humble and nice person in spite of all of his success. Naturally, we gave our client firm the green light to extend him an offer of employment—in fact, the sooner, the better. However, there was one little hitch. Our outstanding job prospect didn't want to go back to Corporate America. Quite the contrary, as if he were having a clandestine affair with another woman, he snuck away early from work three days a week, just before everyone left for the day. Only he wasn't meeting some steamy dish for drinks, but he was taking English literature courses at a small liberal arts college near his office on the outskirts of the city. By the time he got his pink slip, because the company was acquired by an even larger global manufacturing concern, he was ready to realize his lifelong dream—teaching the classics at a parochial high school in the same small town where he and his wife of 30 years had been raised. As my client fumed, this individual took his severance package and spent another 20 years teaching young men and woman to appreciate the value of reading good books. While not a typical example by any means, it is a fascinating one, nonetheless.

Getting Additional Education and Training

The topic of education and additional training is a bit of a dilemma. On the one hand, furthering your education and acquiring the needed credentials required to enter a new profession or keep current in your existing line of work can be essential to you. On the other hand, as will be discussed in detail in Chapter Three, overloading yourself with high levels of credit card or student loan debt from costly vocational programs, which make baseless claims about career riches, can be a very expensive mistake. This problem can be made worse by enrolling in a for-profit vocational school that promises far more than what can be delivered in terms of job opportunities and subsequent career advancement. At this time, however, we will focus on the positive side of going back to school.

Before making the decision to return to the classroom, it is critical that you take several factors into consideration. First, you must evaluate your current skill set as it pertains to performing at a competitive level against comparable peers within your chosen profession. There are several ways in which you can get this kind of critical feedback. First, you might have a pretty good idea of where you are deficient and thus, you are prepared to locate resources to assist you in counteracting these issues. Informally, you might ask some of your former fellow employees if they would provide you with candid feedback on your strengths and weaknesses. The key to obtaining honest feedback, however, is for you to keep quiet and not overreact or respond defensively if you are in disagreement with the message that is being delivered to you. Once you start rationalizing and seeking to justify your behavior, the game is over so to speak, and the quality of candid feedback from the other person will be cloaked in socially desirable terms that will not do you much good. In short, shut up and listen. If you feel the feedback is unfair, examine it in light of other information you receive. If no one makes mention of the faults your one critic has identified, you can probably dismiss the data. On the other hand, if more than one person cites an area for improvement, be ready to listen and develop a plan to address the topic. Finally, an evaluation of your current skills can be obtained at a local community college that offers vocational testing services to assess aptitudes and abilities. Some community resource centers as well as a number of outplacement firms offer similar services.

Second, you should make an honest assessment of your preferred learning style. For example, some people have trouble sitting still in a classroom. Listening to other people giving lectures or explaining materials—which they have to imagine in their heads without actually seeing the work performed—can be difficult. Hence, for these individuals, learning by doing is a better way to approach the subject of interest. This means actually having hands-on experience in a situation where the feedback can be immediate. Finally, there are those people who are self-starters with respect to acquiring information. For them, they would rather find a book or other course-related material and just operate at their own pace. There is no one learning style that is better nor does it necessarily say anything about a person's native intelligence. Just as some people like comedies and others prefer action adventure movies, so it goes with how people will get the most out of a learning experience.

Third, in the event that you are looking to change careers, some kind of additional education along with proper credentials will no doubt be required of you. In fact, it will be very hard to make a career change without the proper credentials, especially if you are interested in teaching or nursing, or becoming an attorney, a social worker, or a psychologist. Even if a special kind of certification is not a barrier for entering your new profession, having the proper training will be essential to getting hired. Before deciding on a career change, however, it is important to have a realistic understanding of the number of job openings in your prospective field. This is a topic for discussion in the next chapter, but it is an important matter to take into consideration before making a huge investment of time and money. Besides understanding the economic fundamentals of supply and demand of your new vocation, you need to do your homework. This means using Internet search engines and the public library to learn as much about your field as possible. Also, talking to current practitioners is strongly advised, and if you have the opportunity to "shadow" a current practitioner during a typical work day or work week, this will be one of the most helpful ways to make a reasoned assessment before taking the plunge to enter an entirely new profession.

In light of our above-mentioned remarks about accumulating unnecessary debt from expensive education and training institutions, there is one low-cost option that can be equally or even more effective in helping you acquire the necessary skills for your career. These are your community colleges. Almost every locale has a community college catering to its residents. Besides the cost advantages of community colleges, there is the added advantage of being in a classroom setting with people of all ages, so that if you are an older returning student your chances of feeling self-conscious will be minimized. The course catalogues at these schools are rather extensive, and in many cases, classes are taught in convenient locations like nearby middle schools and high schools. While these are not the only purveyors of vocational education and training, they are inexpensive, and most importantly, recognized by national accrediting bodies for their curriculum. Again, as will be discussed later, many expensive private schools are not accredited in spite of what their admissions (i.e., sales) offices have to say as they try to recruit you to enroll at their institution.

Ultimately, the decision to return to school is an important investment of time and money. You must determine whether it will be worthwhile to take on this kind of challenge in your life. By performing a cost-benefit analysis along with exploring both the time and financial commitments involved, you will be doing yourself a big favor. When a person is out of work, especially those who are younger—in their 20s and 30s, the temptation to go back to school is enormous. Regardless of your age, however, with so much "free" time on your hands, school is an easy way to feel productive, and it is also a socially acceptable way of spending your days while you are no longer active in the workforce.

Staying Current with Your Field

The notion of staying up-to-date in your chosen profession is an offshoot of the idea of returning to school. However, it still deserves its own heading. For the older employee, many years have passed since you received your initial education and training. While you might hold a degree in your field, the topics taught when you were in school are probably very different than what is being learned by the younger generation. For example, in my case computers were around when I was in college even though my children believe that cave paintings and smoke signals were the predominant communication modes. One of my charming daughters asked how many clay tablets and chisels were required to produce my dissertation. But despite the existence of computers, most of the hardware in my day were mainframes, and the fear of dropping your card deck loomed large. Today, of course, almost everyone who has not been living in a cave uses a personal computer and/or a laptop. Some of us can even manipulate a smart phone, although the speed at which I text message could be the topic for a comedy routine.

Beyond the need to master the newest technology, staying current on the latest trends in your field will avoid the impression that you're "dated." Reading magazines, journals, and periodicals pertinent to your profession will keep you one step ahead of the pack. While you might not totally agree with the trends of the day, at least you should be conversant enough to make your case. When you were employed full-time, you probably had access to these publications courtesy of your last employer. But the annual subscription fees on these publications is rather expensive, so a viable alternative to reading them when you are out of work is to go to your public library. In certain cases, you might need to find a way to gain access to the nearest university library, since these are the places most likely to subscribe to more specialized literature. Finally, a significant number of these publications are available online and can be accessed that way. Regardless of how you obtain this information, it is essential to maintain a competitive edge in a crowded marketplace.

One More Time: Getting Back into Shape Emotionally

In Chapter One, we discussed the topic of whether or not to seek outside help. Certainly, using a trained professional is a valuable way to address the emotional repercussions of being unemployed. The extent and depth of your bad feelings will largely determine if you are a candidate for extra assistance in getting back on your feet. Yet whether you use external assistance or seek to cope with the problems you face on your own, you want to put yourself in a place where you can conduct an effective job search and look at all of your options. And the key to being able to function at your best is to feel good about yourself physically and emotionally. The alternatives discussed in this chapter present a wide range of options that will benefit you on all fronts. While there is no one best way to get back on top emotionally, any one of the approaches mentioned above will be helpful, depending on your needs.

Perhaps, the one thing that allows people to feel good about an experience is to actually see tangible benefits for their actions. This is why certain people gravitate toward professions like sales, where effort and rewards are closely linked. On the other hand, professions where hard work might not lead to results can cause burnout. Sensitive individuals who work with very sick children or the terminally ill are more likely to experience the effects of job burnout even though their cause is so noble. The job search process can be equally debilitating. For example, sending out hundreds of resumes, searching online job boards for hours, and making phone calls to potential networking contacts who never respond back all contribute to a feeling of burnout and exhaustion even though you may be getting more sleep than you have in years or are no longer tied to a commuter train schedule and having to arrive early at an office each day. Added to these sources of stress is the fear of financial ruin and unpaid bills that are piling up on your desk, and you have a surefire way to feel depressed and overwhelmed.

Believe me, if there were a magic wand to wave over this situation and make it go away, I would be the first to let you know. Furthermore, the knowledge that millions of people are in the same boat as you does little to make you feel any better. On the other hand, controlling what you can, such as your waistline or the time you can devote to volunteering your efforts, will be helpful. Doing well in school is another tonic of sorts in the event you elect to return to the classroom. To help you get back into shape emotionally, there are a couple of useful suggestions I can make. First, get yourself into a routine. Wake up at a set time each day and try to perform a regular set of activities on a specified schedule. For example, you might choose to exercise first thing in the morning or at the end of the day. If you are going to school you have a class schedule to follow—the same thing for a part-time job or volunteer work.

Next, set reasonable and realistic goals for yourself. This could include objectives like losing a certain amount of weight over a specified period of time or the number of phone calls and emails you will send each day. Also, the number of networking sessions and social functions you attend could be the goals you set for the week or the month. The hours you volunteer and the projects you undertake should all be connected with achieving tangible outcomes. As we explained previously in the last chapter, when you meet your goals, you need to reward yourself. Maybe it's a day off from exercise or eating a type of food you like even though it adds pounds to your waistline. If you can afford it, purchase a CD of your favorite artist or buy yourself a book for pleasure reading as opposed to self-improvement.

Getting healthy emotionally also means attending to your social needs. Of course, for certain people, being with others is distressing. It might mean endless repeats of the story surrounding your current situation or a rehash of your job search along with unsolicited and perhaps useless job-seeking advice. If you are uncomfortable with large groups of people at this point in your life, restrict your social activities to what is absolutely necessary like family parties and celebrations or networking events. On the other hand, people might be your elixir of life. You might be the kind of person who needs to be in the company of others, so go do it. Join a gym or health club, get out and volunteer your time, or even choose a part-time position with a high degree of social interaction. By way of another illustrative tale, I remember several years ago running into a rather chatty official at the driver's license renewal facility in our community. He seemed different from the other standard bureaucrats who make you wait in long lines and then send you to another longer line because somebody made "a mistake." When I asked him how he ended up in this job, he informed me it was a part-time position that allowed him to get out of the house and talk to people. With his wife employed full time, his children grown and living in other states, he needed an outlet for his social needs. He told me that he has always awakened by 5:30 a.m. each day and by 7:30 a.m., he has read all of the newspapers and then for the rest of the day he is bored out of his mind. Hence, this job fit the bill for him.

In conclusion, there is no magic bullet for staying emotionally healthy during such a difficult time, but trying to remain upbeat, keeping busy, and either limiting or fulfilling your needs for social interaction will help. Finally, stick with your routine and set goals that will make you feel proud of yourself. Remember: if you have been employed in the past and were successful, you will find another situation where you can be just as successful. The key, however, is perseverance and self-discipline.

CHAPTER THREE

Avoiding Costly Mistakes

There are many issues that take precedence in the mind of a job seeker, in particular, one who is out of work. Besides the need to find a job as soon as possible, there is the whole issue of finances. It is indeed a frightening prospect of not having enough money to live while trying to survive on a spouse's income, or worse, no income at all except state-paid unemployment insurance. As a result, carefully conserving one's resources becomes critical. Unfortunately, there are too many instances where the unemployed individual spends money needlessly, all in the interest of improving his prospects for a better life.

This chapter will discuss in detail five major traps that can drain your money and place you in a further financial hole than when you started the job search process. These five pitfalls threaten to exacerbate an already bad financial situation for the bewildered job seeker. The first deals with high-priced career coaches who often prey on the unemployed and make promises that are doubtful at best. Second, even though we have made a case for further education and training, enrolling in an expensive degree program and becoming saddled with student loan debt is very risky. All too frequently, like the expensive and overly optimistic and cheerful career coaches, these schools make claims that never materialize.

Finally, the idea of independence from ever having a boss or being free to run your own business is a compelling idea. In the end, this might be a viable option for someone frustrated by the vagaries of Corporate America, but being your own boss is far from being headache-free. Starting your own business or purchasing a franchise has its pros and cons, but these factors need to be weighed very carefully before committing any significant amount of financial resources to them. In other instances, the unemployed, and in particular, someone who is desperate, often decide to take the plunge and go into business with a friend or relative. Unless this situation is managed with care and sensitivity, lifelong friendships or cherished family relationships can be torn asunder.

High-Priced Career Coaches

It is hard to find information about job search strategies that are consistent. For example, just reading the career section of any Sunday supplement in your city's newspaper is likely to leave even the most self-assured job seeker bewildered and shaking his or her head. One article tells people to speak-up in job interviews, while another warns that such behavior is a turn off to hiring managers. Another article suggests avoiding the HR department altogether, while the next Sunday there is an article published on how HR is your best resource for finding new job opportunities. One article suggests handwritten thank you notes, while another says you will look like a dinosaur if you don't respond back with email. On and on it goes with friendly advice on using the Internet, dressing for success, dealing with difficult interview questions and overly personal inquiries—all appearing each week in the same or different newspaper columns. After a while, it is enough to make people throw their hands in the air in exasperation.

Along with all of this contradictory advice supposedly from the "experts," the latest recession has spawned a cottage industry of those who take advantage of the pain and misery of the unemployed. This is not to dismiss the notion of seeking advice from a qualified professional. At the same time, however, looking to a person who hangs out a shingle as a career coach and a savior suggests caution. In the event you do require outside assistance, there are some steps you should take to ensure that it will be a rewarding experience for you and not just for the person on the other end taking your money.

Before entering into any kind of an agreement with a career coach, think about your goals and objectives for seeking outside advice. For example, are you interested in getting help on your resume? Or perhaps you need advice on using the right search engines on the Internet? Maybe you're looking for tips on how to handle interviews more effectively? Seeking advice on making yourself more marketable, especially if you have not found yourself looking for work in years, is yet another reason to ask a qualified professional for help. As has been said many times before, if you don't know where you're going, you are unlikely to get there successfully.

In sum, think clearly about what you want to achieve if you are going to spend precious financial resources on seeking outside advice. Next, look at your options. Do you have to spend a lot of money getting outside help? For example, in today's economy, there are many non-profit career centers located in communities near where you live that can be utilized for almost next to no cost. These career centers often benefit from the expertise of former HR managers and business executives, retired or still active in business, who can coach you for almost no fee. Moreover, many of these same centers sponsor special classes and seminars that provide training on how to deal with many of the issues you might otherwise look to a career coach to resolve. Many professionals, including the author, are willing to provide pro bono work to help the jobless get back on their feet and do so without charging them for the advice.

In addition, a large number of religious organizations sponsor groups along with one-on-one coaching for the members of their congregations. While many of these groups offer solace and support, there are probably many members of the congregation who have expertise in career coaching and are willing to volunteer their time to assist those in need of their help and advice.

In the event you decide that retaining a career coach is your best available course of action, you need to take certain things into consideration. For the most part, career coaches are not licensed like other professionals in law and accounting as well as in psychology or social work. At the same time, there are networks that professional career coaches can join and even receive certification through. You need to ask the person you are engaging with if he or she belongs to any such group. It is also a good idea to ask for current references and then call them to learn more about the career coach you are seeking to engage. Next, you need to agree on a set of objectives and issues you want addressed, and if possible, how best to measure or determine if these goals are being met. Finally, you should be very clear about the number of sessions you want and the fees being charged to you along with the terms of payment.

While there is no guarantee that the situation will go as planned, by taking some simple precautionary steps, you can prevent a lot of trouble ahead of time. In the event you do encounter problems, especially unethical or suspicious business practices, immediately contact the Better Business Bureau in your community. In fact, you would serve yourself well to go online at the Better Business Bureau's website and check to see if any consumer complaints have been lodged against the person you are about to engage as your career coach. Finally, if verifiable fraud is involved while you are working with that person, you need to contact the proper law enforcement authorities, starting with the police. Hopefully, none of these last steps will ever have to be taken, but forewarned is forearmed.

Going Back to School and Assuming Costly Student Loans

In general, education is a good thing, although there are instances, like anything else, where too much of a good thing can be harmful. In the case of conserving one's finances, education can also present a pitfall as will be explained below. Therefore, it is critical for people to evaluate not only their own needs for additional education and training, but also what benefits the school or institution will confer on them if they elect to enroll and pay the mandatory tuition bill. After all, student loan debt can be rather significant, with little or no hope of paying it down or doing anything more than meeting the interest payments on the debt. Therefore, an individual has to think long and hard about his or her options regarding a return to the classroom.

As noted in Chapter Two, going back to school to retool your skills or learn entirely new ones might be a necessary step in making yourself more marketable. Also in that section of the book, it was suggested that people make use of their local community colleges as a valuable resource for additional education and training. With lower fees and accredited course offerings, these institutions make an excellent choice for the cost-conscious job seeker. At the same time, however, there are other places to gain new skills or brush up on old ones. These other schools can also grant degrees from undergraduate bachelor's degrees to graduate degrees like master's and Ph.D.'s. As a person who possesses more degrees than a thermometer, I am not necessarily against higher education of any kind. But as the old adage says, everyone knows what B.S. stands for and M.S. means more of the same, while Ph.D. means piled higher and deeper.

Professional education and private degree granting schools and institutions are big businesses today. These schools charge students thousands and thousands of dollars to attend classes. In many instances, these classes are online as a way of expanding the convenience of distance learning as well as increasing the marketing base of the school. Many of the degrees that are offered are highly vocation-specific in disciplines such as computer science, nursing, criminal justice, construction management, counseling psychology, and so on. However, before enrolling in such a school, prospective students must have a few important questions adequately answered lest they get taken for a ride, and we're not just talking about enrolling in driving school.

First, is the school accredited and by what accreditation body? There is no sense enrolling in an institution which is not properly accredited so that when you apply for jobs that require accreditation and certification, you are turned away by potential employers. Certainly, no one wants to be informed after all of their hard work to take courses and possibly earn a degree that their credential is virtually worthless. Related to these questions about accreditation and credentialing, it is a wise idea to inquire about the make up of the faculty teaching the courses. Are they academics? If so, what are their degrees? If practitioners are teaching as adjunct faculty, what are their credentials in terms of higher education as well as practical experience? Can these same practitioners possibly arrange internships for you or help you in your job search after graduation?

Second, how long does it take to earn a degree and what percentage of students who enroll are actually awarded a degree? All too often, these professional schools are willing to admit students with almost no barriers to entry, but how many of those who enroll actually graduate with a degree in hand? For example, you might ask people in the admissions office what is the ratio of acceptances to actual graduations. Many of these institutions have been the subject of governmental investigations regarding their practices, and you should do your homework online to determine if the school of your choice is under investigation for its shoddy practices. These schools are often no more than "degree mills" with a reputation for taking students' money or granting them loans at high interest rates but never producing the results they promise.

Third, what are the statistics for recent graduates of the school in terms of job placements and starting salaries? Along this same line, does the school have a placement office with a track record for finding graduates jobs that are decent paying and cover the costs of student loans? Even prior to looking for full-time work, does the school arrange for internships and placements in business and industry in order to provide practical experience to students enrolled in their programs? Many schools are willing to award degrees in glamorous-sounding fields, but are there jobs to match the number of people being awarded diplomas for these fields? It's great to say that you are a counseling psychologist, but with no patients and no professional practice that doesn't amount to much.

Finally, what does it cost to attend the school? Also, is student loan funding available? Far too often, these schools will bury a student in debt as much as $50,000 to $100,000, and there is little if any hope of paying off these staggering amounts of student loan debt because there are no job prospects at the end of the rainbow after the completion of the degree. Perhaps, even more unfortunate is that the jobs available will never pay enough to retire the debt from your student loans, and you'll spend many of your best earning years trying to reduce the balance on the loans you accumulated as a student.

In a word or two, do your homework! Just as you will diligently apply yourself to studying for your degree by being well prepared for your classes, you must utilize those same study skills to investigate the answers to the above-mentioned questions. Your failure to address these issues will be at your own peril, and you will find yourself with a degree that is worth little more than the paper on which it is printed. Remember, the time you spend exploring these matters upfront will pay solid dividends once you have received your degree or certification to enhance your marketability.

Starting Your Own Business

There is no question that many jobless people contemplate the thought of starting their own businesses in the hope of never having to work for someone else ever again. It's a nice idea, but you need to take certain things into consideration. First and foremost, it is not as easy as it looks. Also, do you have the right personality and temperament to be an entrepreneur? The topic of entrepreneurship is a popular one, and there are many books and newspaper articles written on the subject as well as regular dosages of online snippets about being your own boss. Furthermore, there are classes and workshops along with degree granting programs on entrepreneurship. Don't be fooled; not everyone is cut out to run their own business, and start-up costs can be staggering, especially if you are thinking of investing in a lifelong dream of owning a restaurant or starting your own bread-and-breakfast lodge in a popular resort town. In short, these enterprises cost a lot of money.

Before discussing the pitfalls of entrepreneurship, it is important to distinguish the difference between starting a business from scratch and taking your professional skills as a former engineer or human resources administrator and becoming an independent consultant who charges a daily rate. The latter topic is deferred until the end of this chapter because in many ways, it is not as costly a mistake as everything else discussed in this section of the book. In fact, it is one way you can actually earn extra income while you continue with your full-time job search.

Obviously, an entire book could be written (and many have) on the matter of starting your own business, but in the space allotted here, let's look at a couple of key considerations. Number one, if you have never had an itch to be your own boss, it is probably not a good idea to pursue entrepreneurship at this point in your life. For example, do you have the stomach for entrepreneurship? Can you live with the peaks and valleys that accompany the starting and running of your own business operation? Remember, when you are out selling, no income is being generated from the business and conversely, when you are engrossed with the business you are not selling your enterprise's products or services. Finally, to secure a credit line with a bank, you will probably have to collateralize the loan with the deed to your house. Is this what you or your family wants?

Entrepreneurs are probably born and not made. Most people who start their own businesses do so at a young age; in fact, they are often serial entrepreneurs who have opened a number of businesses during their careers. They typically have exaggerated needs for control, and they experience trouble working under anyone else's guidance and supervision. They like to run their own show, and sharing is hard for them. They are exceptionally hands-on and are comfortable without having a sizeable support staff and adequate resources for delegating chores. Do these statements describe you? If not, I wouldn't attempt to start a new business no matter how tempting the idea. Finally, if you have worked inside a larger organization where you have been comfortable with your bosses and also enjoyed the assistance provided to you from having other people available who could help support your work efforts, becoming an entrepreneur is not the best choice for your next career move.

If my gratuitous advice has had no effect on you, then proceed at your own risk, knowing that most start-ups don't live to see their fifth birthday party. Therefore, before starting your business, look very carefully at the costs involved. How much capital will it take to realize your dreams? Where are those funds coming from? The bank? A venture capital fund? Your supportive friends and relatives? All three are viable sources of start-up funding, but you need to know the conditions of repayment and/or the proposed ownership stake in your new enterprise. Perhaps even more critical than the money to support your fledgling operation is a written business plan, which will be required by any lending institution worth its salt.

We could go on and on about the hazards of entrepreneurship (as well as the potential rewards), but suffice it to say that as tempting as the notion is of being an independent operator without a boss to report to each morning, most would-be entrepreneurs forget the most important thing about being your own boss. The truth is, if you want to have a successful business of your own, you are not your own boss. You are everybody else's employee. This means that your customers or your clients are your new bosses, and they can be very demanding in calling the shots. If you can't fathom the thought of satisfying multiple masters, don't even think about starting a new business, no matter how viable your idea.

Buying a Franchise Business

For those who prefer the notion of being their own boss but with the advantage of a turn-key operation, franchising might be a viable option for them. Very often, companies letting people go will offer buyout packages, especially for those at the executive level to those employees who have been with the organization for many, many years. For individuals in this latter group, the final buyout number offered by a former employer can be quite attractive as well as substantial. Since purchasing a franchise operation can be rather expensive, these are good sources of funds for your down payment. But before taking all that hard-earned cash and spending it in one place, especially on a franchise operation, you need to be careful and again do your homework. Finally, the same sources of funds that can be tapped to start a business are also available for purchasing a franchise.

The cost of purchasing the rights to a franchise operation can vary tremendously. For example, they can be as low as $25,000 to $50,000 to several hundreds of thousands of dollars depending on the franchise organization. This book in no way purports to evaluate which franchise operations are good bets and which ones should be avoided. On the other hand, just as in starting your own business, you need to ask some rather pointed questions. To start with, you must assess all of the costs involved in purchasing a franchise and not just the licensing and start-up fees. What about revenue sharing along with the costs for the maintenance and repair of the facility? For example, if renovations are needed, who pays?

Additionally, what kind of training and support will you receive from the franchise? Are there extensive classes? Are they in a classroom or online? Will you be supplied with manuals outlining standard operating procedures? How much leeway will you be allowed to run your own franchise operation versus conforming to strict operating guidelines? Apart from those, there are other issues as well. For example, will you have exclusive rights over a prescribed geographical territory? Or will the franchise allow another person or persons to open an identical business to yours within a short distance of your store that then competes for your hard-earned customers? Does the franchise have the right to buy you out for any reason such as the business has become very successful and now the franchise owners want to take over? Finally, what are the reasons the franchise can close your business, and has this kind of a situation occurred before? If so, when and where?

The last things to consider before entering into a franchise agreement relate to our earlier questions about your suitability for running your own business. In this case, however, there are the added questions about your willingness and ability to supervise other people immediately as opposed to building your business carefully over time. Have you spent your entire career as an individual contributor? If you have been given supervisory responsibility, have your direct reports been self-starters or professionals, like other accountants or highly motivated sales representatives? In running a franchise you will probably find yourself managing a workforce of entry-level, younger employees, for whom tardiness and attendance might prove to be a challenge. Moreover, if you supervised a small group of people, maybe two or three individuals, are you up to the task of doubling or tripling that number?

Like starting your own business, buying a ready-made franchise is not necessarily the road to riches. You need to weigh a number of factors into the equation in order to determine if this is the right choice for you. If it isn't a wise decision, then you might just waste a lifetime's worth of retirement funds chasing an elusive dream.

Going into Business with Friends or Relatives

The pitfalls of this next topic are probably fairly obvious to most people, but nevertheless, it is a tempting option if certain stars are in alignment. For some people, they have relatives who run successful businesses, or they may come from a family that owns a business, but for one reason or another, they have elected to work elsewhere. Suddenly, with no job or immediate job prospects to support you and your family, relatives begin beckoning you to jump on the bandwagon. In other instances, you have friends and acquaintances who you've always admired and gotten along great with who are talking with you about realizing your dreams of being in business together. Certainly, there are many success stories that point to friends and relatives making a successful go of it, but be careful, because the case files are equally full of stories about such relationships that fail, and the fallout can be very damaging.

One of the major problems with going into business with friends or relatives is that personal feelings and emotions can cloud a person's judgment rather easily. For example, do you want to tell your sister that her husband is ill-equipped to run the sales operation? Do you want to have a confidential talk with your former college roommate about how he is not careful enough with keeping records and that your business might get into trouble in the event of an IRS audit? Believe me, these kinds of discussions are difficult enough with strangers or people with whom you have less emotional or personal attachment, yet alone a relative or close friend.

Even if relationships between relatives and friends never reach the stage of a potential confrontation as discussed above, things can go wrong with your business. Are you prepared to ask your uncle to take a pay cut in his overly generous salary so that the business can meet its payroll and other overhead obligations? What if your best friend's wife is sick or has a child with special needs, and you have to ask that person to forego a bonus because you had a bad year or you are anticipating reduced revenues the next year and you need to conserve funds? Finally, would you have the backbone to tell your father that it is time for him to step aside and let the next generation run the business?

In the end, when a business deal goes bad with a friend or relative, you not only lose money, but you could very well lose a valued relationship. The idea of seeing your cousins at family functions and having to avoid them because of hard feelings is not a comforting thought. What about that lifelong friend from high school with whom you played sports and who went to the same college with you? Can you live with losing that friendship? All of these examples are well-documented and real, and they are the direct fallout of poor judgment to enter into a business relationship with a friend or relative. In short, this is an option for financial rewards that perhaps carries an even greater risk than the other two discussed in this chapter.

Distinguishing between Starting a Business and Being a Consultant

In the spirit of ending on a positive note, let's talk about a type of business venture that lacks many of the financial risks and high costs and expenditures associated with the others we have discussed thus far. Starting a consulting or advisory business, especially if you are a credentialed professional, is a relatively low-cost and risk-free way to earn needed income and possibly launch yourself into it for a full-time career. The start-up overhead costs for a consulting business can be next to nothing, especially if you work from home. With today's smart phones, Internet access, and various technological tools, you can run your business from almost anywhere, even when you're on vacation.

It is easier to launch a consulting business if you have been moonlighting your services even before losing your job. For example, if you are an accountant who has helped people navigate and successfully complete their tax forms, this is a natural segue for starting your own tax preparation and accounting business. If you are a contractor or a tradesperson who has helped others with do-it-yourself projects, then starting a small contracting business is natural. After all, with both of these examples, you have a ready-made group of referrals, and in spite of all the Internet and social networking that occurs in our world today, word-of-mouth is still probably the most potent form of getting new business.

Another source of both leads and income is, of course, to teach a course at a local community college or in a high school extension program that allows you to transmit your knowledge to people who are interested in what you do. The income from teaching will supplement your budget at home, and by exposing others to what you know and have gained over a lifetime of work in a particular field or profession, you will get the word out about your knowledge and expertise which will likely help generate leads for your new business. The only thing that you are spending to teach is your time as opposed to the start-up costs to open a new business.

Nevertheless, starting a low-budget, low-overhead consultancy has its pitfalls, especially if your long-term goal is to find another full-time job. While it is probably naïve to think that you will have the luxury of scheduling consulting work on your own terms, you should try at least to budget your time in order to continue your job search. Again, as in the case of starting a new business from scratch, time spent selling or marketing is not earning you income, and time spent on billable work takes away from prospecting for new accounts. In the proverbial case of a poverty of riches, one-person consultancies occasionally lock (or luck) into long-term contracts with companies as these organizations sometimes seek to outsource certain services, and you as an independent consultant can be trapped into a situation where you are no longer available to pursue an intensive job search, and thus, you might miss out on some excellent opportunities with long-term implications.

Clearly, selling yourself as a consultant has its plusses and minuses. My own sense is that there are probably more advantages to such a situation than disadvantages. Besides making some extra money from the process, consulting allows people to stay active and remain sharp in their chosen field. One of the serious drawbacks to today's long-term unemployment is that people are losing their edge as their skills atrophy or if they have not kept up with the latest professional knowledge and technologies. By having to either teach a class in your area of expertise or consult for a company requesting your help, you will want to offer state-of-the-art advice to those who are paying to hear you in class or work alongside you at their places of employment. In the end, this is a very viable option to weather long-term unemployment at any age, but especially if you are an older job seeker.

CHAPTER FOUR

What Employers Are Really Looking for

Part of the premise for this book is based on the workshops and seminars our firm has presented during the past decade to help unemployed individuals deal with the maze of finding a new job. The author was originally asked to speak to these groups about the view from the other side of the desk in terms of what do trained business or industrial psychologists look for when they are evaluating a candidate's suitability for a particular position within an organization. The workshop coordinators specifically requested a listing of the most important key factors or dimensions that define consistent success in the workplace.

Over the course of our work, we have identified a dozen common dimensions used by most organizations, to include businesses and not-for-profit agencies, in order to evaluate the competence and suitability of potential job applicants. Some organizations use fewer than these twelve, while other organizations use more. It has been our experience over the past thirty years, however, that most companies use a variation of this list. It is also important to note that these twelve dimensions defining success in most jobs are not mutually exclusive or independent of one another. Instead, there are many instances of overlap. For example, showing a positive attitude pervades several dimensions, to include impact and self confidence, communications and interpersonal skills, and of course, work attitude and leadership.

Meanwhile, leadership itself can be observed in a group setting as well as in supervisory roles.

In the ensuing material in this chapter, each dimension is briefly defined and then followed by a list of questions that more clearly define success according to each dimension. These are questions that people in my firm ask or seek to confirm when evaluating prospective candidates for particular positions at various client companies. These same questions also form the basis of the Interviewer Skills Workshops we offer to people in HR and other related fields in order to improve their ability to evaluate talent in a more effective fashion. In short, this is the view from the other side of the desk. Therefore, you are urged to conduct your own self-evaluation on each of these dimensions to determine exactly where you stand, and more importantly, to explore how you perceive your attractiveness or marketability as a candidate to a prospective employer.

Unfortunately, as politically incorrect as it might sound, most employers focus on two factors more than any others—personal appearance and impact along with verbal communications skills. In sum, if you look good and talk a good game, you have a better chance of being hired than someone who is not so attractive or gifted with his or her words. For certain roles, these two factors are very important. In particular, when a person needs to make a strong first impression in order to get a foot in the door such as in cold calling in sales jobs or for individuals who will be presenting formally in front of other people, the impression that they leave often makes a difference on whether a company offers them a job or rejects their application. Furthermore, as will be seen below, these two factors are important, but there are other dimensions of behavior that predict even more effectively for success on the job. Regardless, appearance and the gift of gab probably count for more than hiring managers care to admit.

In the material presented below, each dimension will be defined and will be followed by a set of self-assessment questions which more clearly define the specific behavior(s) that employers look for when evaluating an applicant on a particular dimension. You can then compare how you fare and, where possible, make the kinds of adjustments that will improve your chances of being hired by an employer. The first ten major dimensions are listed below. They are then followed by two other specialized dimensions—sales and service orientation along with leadership aptitude and ability that only pertain to jobs where a person is selling or supervising. If neither skill is required by a particular position, then it becomes a moot point in terms of evaluating a candidate.

The Ten Most Common Dimensions

- Personal Appearance and Impact
- Self-Confidence and Maturity
- Professionalism
- Communication Skills
- Interpersonal Skills and Cooperation
- Planning, Organizing, and Time Management
- Results-Orientation
- Initiative and Work Attitude
- Responsiveness to Direction and the Ability to Manage Upward
- Tolerance for Frustration

The Two Specialized Dimensions

- Service and Sales Orientation
- Leadership Aptitude and Ability

Personal Appearance and Impact

Impact involves critical factors such as the appearance, personal hygiene, and the self-presentation of the candidate. In face-to-face interactions such as job interviews, this is the very first factor that will influence an employer. Since memory is driven in part by the twin effects of primacy (an individual's first impression of a person) and recency (an individual's last impression of that same person), it is important to make a positive first impression. The topic of personal appearance and impact includes the following questions for consideration:

- Attire, grooming, and personal hygiene:

  o Are you neat and well groomed?
  o Does your manner of grooming and dressing detract from your potential impact as a prospective job applicant (e.g., unkempt hair, excessive perfume or cologne, flashy jewelry, etc.)?
  o Are you in professional attire (e.g., business suit or business wear)?
  o Are you in casual but neat attire (e.g., slacks, sweater, dress shirt, blouse, etc.)?
  o Are you in inappropriate attire (e.g., overly casual manner of dress)?

- Impact and demeanor:

  o Do you come across with presence and impact?
  o Do you look like a person who would fit into the organization?
  o Do you shake hands with the people you meet?
  o Do you smile and try to act positive?
  o Are you open and honest in providing information?
  o Do you project an approachable image?

- Additional defining factors that might influence your initial impact:

  o For example, are you prompt versus late?
  o If you will be tardy, do you call ahead of time?
  o Do you offer a valid reason for being late for the interview?

Self-Confidence and Maturity

Self-confidence pertains to a person's poise and overall demeanor. It is obviously important if you as a candidate are energetic, alert, and able to project an air of confidence in your capabilities. Clearly, there is a fine line here in that showing too much confidence or an abundance of self-assurance will cause you to come across as arrogant or cocky. Maturity is equally important. While the older worker over age forty might scoff at this dimension, we measure maturity not by chronological age but by a person's willingness to take responsibility for his or her actions. In short, maturity is the willingness to hold one's self accountable. The topic of self-confidence and maturity includes the following questions for consideration:

- Do you show the right kind of attitude as demonstrated by your behavior in an interview situation?

  o   Are you energetic versus lethargic?
  o   Are you alert and attentive versus lackadaisical (e.g., slouched in chair)?
  o   On the other hand, are you too energetic (e.g., overly talkative, fidgety, and prone to distracting gestures)?
  o   Do you project an attitude and demeanor that will be perceived as pleasant, personable, and respectful during the interview?
  o   Or are you more likely to come across as negative and aloof?
  o   Overall, do you maintain appropriate eye contact?

- Do you come across as confident and self-assured in your demeanor?
- Or do you come across as boastful and overly confident?
- Are you overly circumspect and self-protective about your past behavior?

  o   Are you willing to admit mistakes and take responsibility for your role in those mistakes?

    o   Or are you quick to lay the blame onto other people for your setbacks and disappointments?

Professionalism

Meanwhile, professionalism addresses whether the candidate has demonstrated consistency, integrity, and business maturity. While certain individuals might think that professionalism only pertains to people who work in recognized professions like law, accounting, or medicine, this is really a dimension that applies to any occupation from sales to the supply chain and operations. Moreover, people who move jobs frequently because they are bored or have lost "their passion" for their work are unlikely to rate highly on this dimension. The notion of professionalism includes the following questions for consideration:

- Have you demonstrated professionalism during the course of your career?

  o   What has been your average job tenure and job stability?
  o   Has your length of tenure increased or decreased with each subsequent job?
  o   Will the reasons cited for your job changes be perceived as plausible?
  o   If you have switched jobs several times, how many of those changes have been driven by the realities of today's economy (e.g., mergers and acquisitions, plant closings, outsourcing, etc.)?
  o   Have you completed the required classes or certifications relevant to your line of work?

- Have you demonstrated ethical behavior during your career?

  o   Have you faced certain temptations and been able to resist them, when, in fact, others haven't acted so ethically?

- o   Can you talk about situations where you have had to make tough decisions, which sacrificed the expedient for the long-term reputation of your career and your organization?

- Are you able to project an image of being positive, altruistic, honest, and sincere?

  - o   Are your values in alignment with those of the hiring organization (e.g., service-oriented, growth-oriented, principled and ethically based)?
  - o   Are you able to talk positively about previous places of employment?
  - o   Or are you inclined to complain about prior jobs and previous coworkers?
  - o   Will you show an ability to place the needs of customers and clients first as opposed to looking out for number one?

- Is your use of language professional during the interview, or do you indulge in profane and inappropriate language?
- Are you prone to dropping the names of others as a way to impress an interviewer?
- Do you have the capacity to demonstrate discretion in describing sensitive matters regarding other people and previous employers? In short, are you given to gossip?

Communication Skills

Along with a person's poise and appearance, the ability to express one's self well in a one-on-one situation or in a group setting during the interview process weighs heavily (sometimes too heavily) in the final decision to extend an individual a job offer. This dimension looks into the candidate's ability to speak clearly, persuasively, and sound convincing as well as listen carefully to others. This dimension also delves into the candidate's ability to communicate effectively with people, both inside and outside of the organization. Finally, the applicant's ability to communicate his or her thoughts in writing is another important part of this dimension. The topic of communication skills includes the following questions for consideration:

- Oral communications:

  o Do you communicate with clarity, or do you struggle with expressing your thoughts and ideas?
  o Are you reasonably articulate?
  o Do other people readily follow your train of thought when you are speaking on a particular topic?
  o Are you convincing and compelling in trying to make a case for your point of view?
  o Do you speak at a good pace, or do you talk too quickly, making it hard to understand what you are trying to say?
  o If English is your second language and the company conducts the majority of business in English, are you able to express your thoughts with sufficient clarity?
  o Do you tend to be wordy and verbose?

    ▪ Are you given to going off on tangents?
    ▪ Do you digress from the topic at hand and then forget the specific question you are being asked?

  o Are you able to project an energetic, enthusiastic, and engaging tone of voice?
  o Are you able to speak with impact and persuasiveness so that others are inclined to listen to your words?

- Do you demonstrate good listening skills? Or are you prone to frequently interrupting and talking over other people?

- Are you inclined to express your thoughts using business-speak and silly-sounding jargon to excess as a way of trying to impress other people?

    o When using industry-related terms, to include acronyms and abbreviations, do you show consideration and take the time to explain those terms?

- How do you prefer to communicate with people inside and outside of the organization?

    o Is your preference for face-to-face communications?
    o Or by email and voicemail?
    o Are you flexible enough to adapt your preferred way of communicating to accommodate your managers and/or your customers?

- Written communications:

    o Are you able to write clearly so that others can understand your words without having to ask for clarification?
    o Are your written materials well organized and easy to comprehend?
    o Based on your written samples, will your writing be seen as too verbose versus well formulated, organized, succinct, and to the point?
    o Will your reader discover glaring problems with spelling, grammar, or misuse of language and phrases?

Interpersonal Skills and Cooperation

This dimension examines the candidate's ability to work with and assist others; it addresses the ability to work cooperatively with peers.

With so many organizations requiring people to function on teams and work on joint projects—even if they are remotely situated from one another—this is an important dimension predicting a person's long-term success. Surprisingly, this dimension is also relevant to people serving in individual contributor roles. Such commonly displayed work behaviors as flexibility, patience, tolerance for others, and competitiveness are also addressed under the heading of interpersonal skills and cooperation. The subject of interpersonal skills and cooperation includes the following questions for consideration:

- Interpersonal style

  o   Do you come across as positive, engaging, and likeable?
  o   Or do you tend to be distant and reserved?
  o   Are you pessimistic and negative?
  o   Overall, are you more of an extrovert or an introvert?
  o   If you are an introvert, can you exhibit an extroverted side to your disposition in order to get along in group-oriented situations?
  o   If you are an extrovert, can you tone it down when working in smaller group settings?
  o   Are you able to exhibit a good sense of humor?
  o   Conversely, do you exhibit an inappropriate sense of humor (e.g., make jokes at the expense of others, excessive sarcasm, overly pointed remarks, or sexual innuendos)?
  o   Do you tend to initiate humor, or are you a person who tends only to appreciate it?

- Are you overly competitive?

  o   Can you work collaboratively with others?
  o   Do you hoard information at the expense of your peers in order to make yourself look better in the eyes of other people, in particular, your bosses?
  o   Do you view success as a zero-sum game with clear-cut winners and losers?

- Are you a team player?

  o Are you flexible and able to adapt to other people's styles for the greater good of the group?
  o Are you accommodating and supportive of others' ideas?
  o Do you freely share recognition and give credit when and where it is due?
  o Do you make an effort to be available in order to assist your coworkers?

- Where appropriate, do you attempt to assert leadership behaviors in the presence of peers?
- Do you seek to draw unnecessary attention to your behavior in a group setting? Would your peers describe you as a "show-off"?
- Do you hold strong beliefs and opinions, which you readily share with coworkers whether your views are solicited or not?
- Past coworker experiences:

  o How would you describe relationships with your current and past coworkers (e.g., positive, cooperative, and respectful versus distant or negative)?
  o How would you describe your least preferred coworker? (Note: The individual that you describe probably has more in common with you than you would like to think)
  o Have you engaged in a significant number of arguments with your coworkers in the past?
  o How have you typically dealt with conflict and disagreement?

Planning, Organizing, and Time Management

As in most jobs, it is important to have a system for organizing and managing a person's time. This dimension examines the candidate's ability to set goals and priorities as well as manage time efficiently and effectively in order to complete tasks and assignments successfully. How a person deals with emails and meetings is also a component of one's ability to manage time. Without the ability to plan and organize, it is often very hard for a person to execute for results or be seen as terribly effective in his or her work assignments. The topics of planning, organizing, and time management include the following questions for consideration:

- Do you have a specific method for organizing your time?
- Do you create "To Do" lists?

  - Do you rank items on the list in terms of importance and prioritization?
  - How do you determine what is a high priority item or task?
  - Do you prepare lists on a consistent basis?
  - What timeframe do the lists entail (e.g., daily, weekly, rolling, or on an as-needed basis)?
  - If using a daily list, how many items are typically on the list?
  - If using a daily list, how many items are typically completed at the end of each day?
  - Is the list paper-based or electronic or both?
  - To what extent are you using Post-It notes? Are they prone to getting lost or misplaced?

- Are you able to utilize helpful technology to stay organized such as a PDA device and/or specific software programs?

  - Do you make use of an electronic calendar to schedule appointments?
  - Are meeting notes and other notations organized and maintained in electronic files?

- How many work-related emails do you typically receive on average each workday?

  - Of those emails, what percentage requires a follow-up?

o   Do you allot specific times during the day to check email, or do you respond immediately to each message as it's received?

o   How much time would you guess that you spend each day—to include your afterhours—reading and responding to incoming emails?

• Are you prone to distractions and interruptions? Do you experience difficulty maintaining your focus?

o   Do you check email continuously throughout the day?

o   What about spending too much time chatting with other coworkers?

o   Are you prone to multitasking and attempting to do too many things at once?

o   Do you confuse multitasking with being effective as well as being viewed as flexible and responsive to the needs of other people?

• How much of your time is spent in meetings each week?

o   Are these meetings that you lead?

o   What kind of preparation time is required for these meetings?

o   How much of your time each day is required for follow-up activities resulting from these meetings?

• Is your work area and desk neat?

• Are you the kind of person who requires an administrative assistant to help you stay neat and organized?

• On an old fashioned one (low) to ten (high) scale, how would you rate yourself with respect to your ability to stay organized and manage time effectively?

• In what areas, in particular, might you stand to improve your planning and organizing skills when it comes to managing time more effectively?

Results Orientation

It is also important to evaluate the candidate's results orientation, not only for sales-related roles, but also for any job assignment where it is important to get things done in a timely and conscientious manner. In sales, for example, placing the wrong person in a territory even for a short time has serious implications for both revenue growth and customer relations. In other jobs, a lack of urgency will slow down critical operations and cause a failure to meet deadlines. In a difficult economy, it will be critical to demonstrate your ability to generate results for the top line (revenue) or the bottom line (cost savings). As such, this dimension addresses whether the candidate is motivated and driven to meet goals. The concept of results orientation includes the following questions for consideration:

- Does your resume reveal specific and tangible metrics as opposed to a simple list of duties and responsibilities that might be found in a standard job description?

  o When given goals and objectives, what has been your track record for success in achieving those outcomes?
  o If working in sales, what percentage of time have you either met or exceeded your sales plan or quota?
  o Again, if working in sales, have you won any awards or recognition for sales efforts (such as the President's Club)?
  o What about any special awards or distinctions you might have received for outstanding achievement at your company?
  o Have there been cost savings associated with your jobs? If so, what were they?

- Are you a competitive individual who likes to win and achieve goals?
- Will your competitiveness prevent you from sharing information and best practices that will lead to other people being successful in their jobs?

- Finally, if you have no previous work-related experience, have you demonstrated the ability to achieve results outside of work such as in school, religious, or community activities?

Initiative and Work Attitude

This dimension examines the candidate's willingness to do things without being asked. It also pertains to motivation and self-discipline and the ability to take seriously one's duties and responsibilities along with one's obligations to work. As such, it is important to discuss prior work experience with regard to tenure and general work attitude. If the candidate is younger and has had limited work experience, then it is important to discuss the person's educational accomplishments and extracurricular activities. Moreover, if the candidate has been out of the workforce for a significant amount of time (e.g., raising a family), then it is important to discuss activities related to community and service organizations. These subjects of initiative and work attitude include the following questions for consideration:

- Have you been promoted on a regular basis, advancing in job responsibility over the years?
- What would you list as your two or three major accomplishments?
- Have you been able to demonstrate consistency and dependability throughout your employment history?

  o For example, how many days a year have you called in sick?
  o On average, how many times a year have you been tardy?

- Attitude toward work:

  o Are you able to show a positive attitude toward previous jobs, or are you inclined to complain about your previous places of work?

- o Have you demonstrated a willingness to make sacrifices for the employer (e.g., put in long hours, handle excessive travel demands, or a willingness to perform business on personal time)?
- o Have you made it a habit trying to cut corners or failing to follow directions properly in order to get through your work more quickly?

- Are you more task-focused than relationship-oriented?
- Motivation and commitment:

  - o Are there specific metrics that can attest to your ability to achieve tangible results for an employer?
  - o Have you shown a tendency toward behaving in a selectively motivated character toward certain aspects of the job?

    - Are you more eager and ambitious when performing tasks that interest you specifically?
    - Are your needs for variety so high that you will experience difficulty completing the more routine aspects of the job (e.g., paperwork, filling out forms, and repetitive tasks)?
    - Are there specific tasks you simply would prefer to avoid in performing work assignments?

- Initiative and ambition:

  - o Can you cite specific examples where you have shown a willingness to show initiative, especially when other people avoided the situation for one reason or another?
  - o Will you consistently go above and beyond what is expected, or are you inclined to perform just the bare minimum?
  - o Do you feel a sense of entitlement so that you push for promotion at the earliest opportunity?

Responsiveness to Direction and Ability to Manage Upward

Since most organizations are hierarchal in structure, this critical dimension delves into your past and present relationships with authority figures in a business setting. Moreover, from our perspective, most people who have been terminated from their jobs have not shown an ability to work successfully with immediate superiors. As such, this dimension addresses the candidate's ability to handle supervision and input from one or more bosses. While the notion of relating well to those in positions of authority has not been very popular in our society since the 1960s, it is nonetheless an important factor in determining who fails and who succeeds in an organizational setting. The idea of managing upward and showing the willingness and ability to be responsive to direction and authority includes the following questions for consideration:

- Overall, what has been your attitude toward authority and authority figures during the course of your career?
- What kind of manager brings out the best in you?
- Conversely, what type of boss would cause you the most difficulty in reporting to and working with on a regular basis?
- Preference of a boss:

  o Will you function better with greater autonomy and freedom in the performance of your tasks and assignments?
  o Can you function independently and work for a boss in a remote location?
  o Or will you be uncomfortable without well-defined expectations and without clear guidance and direction?
  o If you are a person who dislikes "micromanagement," how would you define the term exactly?
  o Can you tolerate close supervision in an open area with your immediate supervisor sitting just a few desks away?
  o Do you prefer to work for a boss who is available to meet on a regular basis?

o Do you prefer to work for a manager who will be honest and straightforward to you?

- How do you prefer to communicate with your managers (e.g., face to face, emails, or voicemails)?
- How willing are you to adapt to your manager's preferred method of communication if it is required of you?
- Ability to accept critical feedback and criticism:

    o Are you overly sensitive or defensive in the face of critical feedback aimed at your performance?
    o Can you cite or draw upon specific examples of where you have incorporated criticism and constructive feedback, which has resulted in significant improvements in your performance and behavior at work?

Tolerance for Frustration

Since every job seems to have its own sources of stress depending on the occupation, this dimension is of critical importance as it discusses the applicant's ability to cope with job stress. In addition, it also addresses the candidate's tolerance for rejection and frustration. This dimension is important because under conditions of stress and frustration, the problematic elements of a person's personality are more than likely to emerge and become magnified. Finally, this dimension is also quite helpful in making reasonably accurate predictions about how long a person will likely stay with his or her job in an organization. The topic of tolerating stress and frustration includes the following questions for consideration:

- What would you describe as your primary sources of stress in the workplace?
- Are there certain types of people who contribute to your sources of stress in the workplace?

- Have you been in the habit of personalizing setbacks and disappointments during the course of your career?
- Have you been able to learn specific lessons from your past mistakes? If so, what were some of those lessons?
- Have you shown an inclination to give up when things get difficult for you?
- In the event that mistakes are made, will you be critical of others and seek to place the blame on them?
- How much responsibility are you able to assume for errors and mistakes without becoming defensive?
- Have you demonstrated the ability to show flexibility in making last-minute requests and shifts in priorities?
- Are you the kind of individual who is motivated by the stress of meeting deadlines, numbers, and sales goals?
- Do you engage in hobbies that help you cope better with stress, allowing you an opportunity to relax outside of work (e.g., sports, exercise, reading, crafts, socializing with family and friends, etc.)?
- What is your current job tenure? (Frequent job changes may indicate that an individual will be quick to leave a position if it does not meet the person's expectations).
- What are the kinds of things that might make you want to quit a job or at least take out your resume and start circulating it around in search of another position?

Specialized Dimensions for Sales Only

Service and Sales Orientation

This dimension is utilized to evaluate candidates applying for sales positions. In certain roles, sales might be a part of the job. For example, in roles where a person must persuade others to accept certain proposals such as in consulting jobs or staff-level positions, this dimension or some variation of it might be used. In general, this area addresses the candidate's willingness to meet the needs of external customers, and in some instances, internal customers. The subject of sales and service orientation includes the following questions for consideration:

- How would you describe your approach to selling?

  o Can you provide examples to demonstrate how your preferred approach to selling has been effective?
  o Are you relaxed and laidback in your approach to selling?
  o Are you comfortable and willing to push the products and services sold by your employer?
  o Do you know how to close and when to ask for the sale?
  o Will you likely be perceived as a pest by being overly persistent with customers and clients?
  o How would you describe your use of a consultative approach to selling products or services?
  o How would your customers evaluate your listening skills?

- What specific steps do you take to connect personally with your customers?
- In terms of dealing with customers, are you willing to probe for answers?

  o Will you be perceived as approachable and open to answering questions?
  o Are you the type of person who is likely to be too intimidated to ask your customers or clients sensitive questions?
  o Conversely, will customers be too intimidated to ask you certain questions?
  o Are you willing to follow up with customers and remain in contact with them after completing a sale or even in cases where you have dealt with rejection during a sale?

- How would you evaluate your ability to follow up on requests as well as follow through on commitments?
- Are you likely to be perceived as trustworthy and credible by your customers?
- Do you tend to overpromise and under-deliver or the other way around (under-promise and over-deliver)?
- Are you able to be accommodating and willing to sacrifice your personal time afterhours or on weekends in order to service your clients?

    o Can you provide specific examples where you have made sacrifices of your own personal time in order to service a customer?

- In what other ways have you demonstrated a commitment to servicing your customers or clients?
- Would you describe yourself as reactive versus proactive in your approach to customer-service issues?

    o If you see yourself as proactive, are there specific examples where you have taken the initiative on behalf of the customer?

Specialized Dimensions for Supervisors and Managers Only

Leadership Aptitude and Ability

This critical dimension is evaluated for positions that require leadership in managing and directing the efforts of other people. It looks into the candidate's leadership style and the person's ability to guide the work of others. While no one leadership style is considered superior to any other approach, any candidate who is under consideration for a role with supervisory and leadership responsibility must be able to demonstrate tangible evidence through specific, real-life examples of why he or she is worthy of a such a trusted position in their organization. The whole notion of leadership aptitude and ability includes the following questions for consideration:

- Have you had prior leadership experience?
- If yes, for how many years have you been responsible for directing the efforts of other people?
- On average, how many individuals have you supervised?
- Have you ever asked or been asked to relinquish your supervisory responsibility? If so, for what reasons?
- Have you ever voluntarily relinquished a leadership role? If so, for what reasons?
- How would you best describe your leadership style?

    o Leadership by example
    o Situational leadership
    o Leadership through expertise and experience
    o Charismatic leadership
    o Relationship-orientated leadership
    o Task-focused leadership

- Have others ever described you as a difficult and demanding boss? If yes, why?

    o Are you prone to micromanaging?
    o In delegating assignments downward to employees, are you the kind of manager who makes unnecessary work for other people?
    o Have you been characterized as overly direct and blunt in delivering feedback to your staff?
    o Will employees seek to avoid you and characterize you as unapproachable?

o   Are you the kind of person who is so busy attending meetings and other matters pertaining to your agenda as to be seen as unavailable?

o   Have you shown an inclination toward playing politics in order to improve your own situation or that of your work team?

o   Are you inclined to play favorites with your employees?

• Are you willing to provide your staff with autonomy and freedom in performing their tasks?

o   Will you hold people accountable for their actions?

o   Or will you be more concerned with nurturing relationships and avoiding hurt feelings as opposed to leading others in a firm fashion?

• Are you more inclined to perform better with self-starters—such as professionals or highly technically oriented employees—who are often more likely to be introverted in their approach to working with other people?

• If a hypothetical sample of past and present employees who have reported to you could be gathered into a room, how as a group would they collectively describe your leadership style?

• What advice for improving or changing your approach would they be willing to offer to you?

• Have you ever had a 360-degree feedback survey conducted by your organization in order to assess your leadership style? If yes, what were the results of the 360-degree feedback survey?

PART II

CHAPTER FIVE

Writing Resumes That Get Attention

The next six chapters are aimed at getting you the right job. Even in a highly competitive job environment, it is possible to land a job that meets your needs for interesting work along with a suitable salary to support your family and/or your lifestyle. Much of the focus of these ensuing chapters will be on preparing your resume as well as how to interview effectively, and when called upon to take tests, how to properly handle the questions posed by these tools, which today are typically administered online.

The following information about preparing your resume is intended to position you to get to the next steps with a potential employer that will eventually lead to a job offer. A next step might mean taking an online test or perhaps being invited to the company's offices in order to meet with your prospective coworkers and undergo a series of interviews with them. These onsite visits often start with an interview with a company representative from the human resources department. While much is written negatively about the human resources department, these people are generally highly professional and committed to helping staff their employers with the best possible people. They too are under a lot of pressure as the number of resumes submitted to them increases significantly as unemployment rises. Being curt or abrupt, or worse, condescending with HR or those involved in the hiring process, will serve no one well, in particular, you. In short, it will likely lead to a quick exit from the hiring process.

There are many different ways to write a resume. Fortunately, there are books and manuals for purchase or on file at your local public library. Information is also available online. While hiring a resume writing service might be advisable in certain instances, much of what needs doing in terms of preparing a winning resume can be done by the candidate. In this chapter, we will discuss various resume writing strategies along with some do's and don'ts about preparing a resume for submission. There are, of course, a number of "theories" about writing an eye-catching resume, and as we noted previously, one only has to read the Sunday supplement of your local newspaper that advertises jobs and also dispenses career advice in order to get a wealth of information (and misinformation). As noted, a sizeable portion of that advice tends to be contradictory. One expert tells job applicants to use only action verbs, while another suggests complete sentences. Recommendations abound, but in the end, there are a few key points that reflect a consensus, and naturally, they are no more than simple common sense rules of thumb.

For example, your resume is a reflection of you. It is a work product that will create an initial impression. Obviously, if the resume is sloppy or poorly organized, or worse, contains spelling and grammatical errors, your chances of being called for an interview or invited to proceed in the hiring process will be severely limited. If you are not a careful proofreader—and there are some of us, including yours truly, who fall under this heading—find a person who has a strong attention to detail. Regardless of how vigilant or meticulous you might be, even the most painstaking person will probably miss certain errors or mistakes after having read over the same document (i.e., your own resume) one time too many. Therefore, it behooves even the most conscientious people to have other individuals review their resumes before sending them on to a potential employer.

Possible Points of Contention Regarding Your Resume

The debatable aspects of resume preparation (if one can believe that preparing a resume is cause for such consternation and excitement) involve a couple of key points to be covered below. But before discussing those possible points of contention, let me digress for a moment to talk about the process as it relates to the older, established employee, who has probably not prepared a resume in the past fifteen to twenty years. If you have been steadily and gainfully employed with a single company for all of this time or your company was acquired or merged with another during this same period of time, but fortunately for you your job status was unaffected, you have probably never had to sit down and compose a resume to sell yourself to another employer. Hence, the thought of going through this process can be intimidating. Relax. If you can locate your last resume or one that has been recently updated, you're far ahead of the game. Regardless, there is no magic about preparing a resume. If you must start from scratch, we offer a few helpful hints hopefully to make the process easier.

First, there is the inevitable question about the right length of a person's resume. Should it be condensed to only a page? What about listing all of the jobs in a person's career along with educational accomplishments and possible professional credentials to include certifications, publications, and speaking events like conference presentations? After all, can a job candidate's contributions and accomplishments in the course of an entire career be limited to one page? There is, of course, no simple rule of thumb to follow. In general, however, a resume should convey what you are looking for in a job and exactly why you are qualified to hold such a position of responsibility. If you can summarize such important information on one page, the more power to you. On the other hand, if you need two or three pages to state your case, then do so. The key is that the information presented should be relevant and helpful to the HR representatives and managers making the final hiring decisions.

The advantage of one-page resumes is that when written with key words that are read when scanned through a computer, the likelihood that you will be selected for further consideration by the hiring company is increased significantly. With the added advantage of word processing equipment, you can cut and paste words into your resume, which will aptly be recognized by the scanning programs used by companies to identify the best possible choices to advance in the hiring process. Meanwhile, lengthier resumes allow the job applicant the opportunity to present specific examples, typically through metrics and KPIs (key performance indicators), to verify a person's ability to contribute to a company's bottom line, either through generating revenues or cost-saving initiatives or both. To resolve this dilemma, we suggest the shorter, one-page version for use when it is known that the hiring organization is using some type of scanning software to weed out unacceptable resumes. However, if called by the company for a first round of interviews, it might be better to have on hand a more detailed resume with metrics and KPIs. The key notion in this whole process is to remain as flexible and fluid as possible.

There are several other areas that require clarification with respect to writing a winning resume besides the appropriate length of the document. Many resumes list only the years of employment and omit the month and year together. For example, there are resumes that say a candidate was employed in the XYZ Company from 2006 to 2007. This can be rather misleading. For example, a person might have worked at the XYZ Company for almost two years from January of 2006 until December of 2007. On the other hand, the person might have been hired by the XYZ Company late in December of 2006 and terminated in the first few weeks of January of 2007. That's quite a difference! Of course, a candidate seeking to paint over the latter situation would be inclined to use only years as opposed to including the months that he or she worked for the XYZ Company. While not every job applicant who only cites the years he or she was employed is trying to pull a fast one, it does leave open the possibility that there is more to the story.

Another concern somewhat related to the last matter is the deliberate omission of graduation dates from the resume of an older applicant. The standard thinking is that if a candidate lists the year he or she was awarded a bachelor's degree, the hiring manager can then compute the intervening years from the date of the degree to the present and then add the general number twenty-one in order to arrive at an approximate estimate of the applicant's age. Of course, no one is fooled by this tactic, and it often calls more attention to your age than simply listing the correct date of graduation from college or graduate school. Finally, if the candidate went back to school later in life, the exact year of graduation is probably not such an issue since the hiring manager can see that the person was working a while prior to receiving their college diploma.

Finally, in keeping with our comments about the notion of concealing one's age, we do not suggest limiting the jobs listed on your resume to the last ten or fifteen years. Again, so-called "job experts" say that only the last ten to fifteen years of a person's career are relevant, but that's simply not true. Each individual is a complete body of work, and to truncate your life's experience in the world of work will not benefit you to the extent that the experts imply. If you have a rich history in a field of endeavor, let your future employers know about it. At the same time, if you fear being labeled as "dated" by the length of time you have served in your profession, be sure to include information on your resume about relevant skills and certification, especially those relating to your knowledge and facility with the latest technology and trends impacting your field. On the other hand, if you switched fields completely such as moving from manufacturing into sales or some other profession, then it is okay to summarize those earlier years by stating something along the lines that you worked for the ABC Manufacturing Company between 1975 and 1988 in production and then list your other jobs with either the ABC Manufacturing Company or other organizations that have employed your sales services.

From our perspective, it does not serve the applicant well to try to deceive a potential employer about age or anything else. In the end, honesty is the best policy, and it will work to everyone's advantage to tell the truth. There is no question that everyone wants an edge when at least five people are chasing every job opening advertised today, and there is no question that the competition is fierce. Moreover, as we have stated before, there is no prize or silver or bronze medals for being the second or third choice to fill a particular job opening. But still, trying to rig a resume so that you look years younger will only catch up to you when you meet your prospective employer for the first time. Later in this book, we will talk about how people try to game the system further by faking their personality tests or giving socially acceptable answers during their interview either over the telephone or in face-to-face encounters. Today's human resources professionals along with most hiring managers are well-trained and are able to spot such discrepancies, which in the end will result in your receiving a letter, or more than likely, an email thanking you for your time but telling you that the company is not interested in your services.

To conclude this discussion without beating a dead horse, you are who you are. In the event that you are able to give an academy award performance and fool all of the experts, are you really a winner? As we tell candidates who are evaluated by psychologically based job assessments conducted at our firm, what happens if you put one over on us and the company? More than likely, the truth will make itself known, and the person will prove to be a poor fit for the job. In that case, the individual will likely lose his or her job at some point, typically sooner rather than later. Then what is a person to do? Does he or she conceal the job and avoid listing it on his or her resume by using only years as opposed to months and years as discussed above? Or does the person list this short-term job on his or her resume and then spend every subsequent job interview explaining how he or she managed to get fired in such a brief period of time? Incidentally, for the candidate who thinks it is clever to omit a job altogether by using only years without more specific information, that same short-term job might be found on an Internet search, and then the person will have the humiliating experience of being called into the HR Department and being terminated for falsifying a resume.

Avoid the Job Description Approach

Far too many resumes read like the typical job description that might be found filed with any HR department. In particular, resumes that read like job descriptions enumerate the duties and responsibilities the person has performed in his or her present role or for any other previous positions. For example, the items found on such a resume might read as follows:

- Responsible for the sales and marketing efforts of the entire office products division
- Managed technical resources associated with the corporate Data Center
- Had oversight of all real estate acquisitions for the property management function at the company
- Designed and created Web sites as required using a variety of state-of-the-art tools
- Supervised a staff of audit professionals who perform off-site review of the company's plant operations
- Operated with cross-functional teams to collaborate on branding strategies

Certainly, there is nothing shabby about any of these duties as they reflect major areas of responsibility during the course of a person's career. On the other hand, each of these statements lack specificity about what was accomplished in performing these functions. In short, the above-listed statements are almost exactly the same ones that would be found in the person's job description were the candidate asked to reproduce it for a future employer.

Just a word or two about buzzwords, business speak, or superlatives that have lost their impact from overuse. Statements using such hackneyed terms as "world class," "best practices," or "high performing" no longer pack much punch. Instead, they are often the objects of derision as in-house recruiters and hiring managers sift through stacks and stacks of resumes, each one proclaiming greater feats than the last one. As we will discuss later in the book, about the only thing worse than including these clichéd terms on your resume is using them in your speech!

The only potential benefit in using such an approach of listing specific duties and responsibilities is if, as stated before, the job seeker knows that the company to which he or she is making the application is deploying special scanning software to identify key words and phrases to determine the candidate's match for the advertised opening in the organization. If, however, there is no evidence that such software is in place, then the resume will look dull, and frankly, rather uninspiring.

Use Metrics to Enhance Your Value to an Employer

In today's competitive economy, especially when employers are reluctant to hire, companies want to know specifically what a person can do for the organization in order to help it survive and even prosper despite having to operate in a difficult business climate. This then means providing the proof in the body of a person's resume of having achieved tangible results. Not every job, of course, is designed to generate revenue, but at the same time, most jobs look to save costs and improve profitability in some way. As a result, the following statements within the body of a resume are much preferred:

- Exceeded quota by 20 percent over three consecutive years while working as a field sales rep
- Saved the company $250,000 on outside audit fees by analyzing internal expenses and submitting those figures for verification to an independent group in finance
- Produced fifteen new brochures to support the marketing campaign for the company's latest line of new snack foods
- Reduced waste and expenses from unnecessary copying and duplication by $75,000 through using the company's intranet
- Helped consolidate the company's distribution centers from twelve to five, thereby saving the organization $2.5MM a year in added expenses

- Reduced employee turnover at the company's branch offices from over 33 percent a year to less than 5 percent within the space of two years

For those in the not-for-profit world, there might not be the opportunity to cite revenue generation even though every organization is looking for people who will help save money and reduce unnecessary costs. In this case, here are a few sample statements that would enhance the resume of a person working in the non-profit world:

- Increased membership in the organization by over 200 people a year while serving as the head of the newly created membership services committee
- Facilitated a changeover in the association's membership billing system that reduced annual expenses by $50,000
- Performed an efficiency study of the organization's account payable and reduced the number of required steps that resulted in annual cost savings of $30,000
- Designed and administered eight new in-house training seminars to assist members to function more effectively in supervisory roles
- Consolidate the organizations RFP (request for proposal) process and reduced response time to vendors from 180 days to 30 days
- Hired and staffed three satellite offices in New Haven, Connecticut, Springfield, Missouri, and Boise, Idaho

Clearly, the more strongly you can state your case that you are results-oriented and able to earn your keep so to speak, the more likely any potential employer would be inclined to want to make you a job offer. No matter how dire the financial circumstances any company or not-for-profit company is facing, every organization wants to improve its situation by both raising revenue and reducing expenses. Job candidates with a proven track record for doing either or both will be much more highly sought after in the marketplace.

Consider Using Multiple Formats for Your Resume

Customization is apparent in almost every facet of our lives today. There is a cable channel catering to almost everybody's interests. The same is true for books as well as fashion. We can engage in hobbies and interests that once might be seen as so esoteric that nobody could follow them like the English Soccer Leagues or Southeast Asian cooking. These same principles of customization can also be used to your advantage in conducting your job search. In short, by preparing customized resumes, you can enhance your marketability. Of course, all of these trends are driven by today's technologies. The Internet, search engines, and especially word processing equipment have all added to the convenience of our lives, but at the same time, they have added a layer of complexity to everyday existence as well.

Because each organization is different, with the touch of a few keystrokes, it is possible to alter a resume and customize it for a company looking to fill an advertised vacancy. This means you can change your career objective to more carefully suit the needs of a prospective employer. If key words are likely to get your foot in the door, you can make sure that they are added accordingly. For those employers who will likely be more impressed with your specific accomplishments in terms of money saved or revenue generated, you can change your resume format to meet those needs with specific indicators of your ability to contribute to the organization. Finally, it might serve you well if you use two resume formats for the same employer. For example, one format might contain the key words that will help separate your resume from the crowd when submitted for scanning by special software programs. In the event you are asked to meet with the representatives of the company onsite, you can then bring along a slightly different document reflecting all of the goals you have accomplished at your previous places of work.

Certainly, the whole notion of customization applies to cover letters as well. The standard "To Whom It May Concern" will get you nowhere today and will probably lead to a quick trip to the rejection pile. Again, with the advantage of the Internet and today's search engines, it is possible to conduct research on any potential new employer. By digging deep and finding a tangible connection between your background and the company that interests you, you can compose a more compelling cover letter that will very likely get the attention of the in-house recruiter or the hiring manager. As we will discuss in the next chapter, there is absolutely no reason for you to be uninformed or unprepared for any encounter with a prospective employer.

In closing, while the resume might seem like a mere formality to be written and emailed or snail-mailed, it is, for better or worse, the proverbial first foot in the door, which will determine how far you, as a job candidate, will proceed in the hiring process.

CHAPTER SIX

Doing Your Homework

Vignette: "Ooops, I forgot who signed my check"

Not long ago, our firm was looking for extra help on a contract basis (so what else is new in today's economy), and we put out the word to the professional community. To no one's surprise, we received a rather substantial amount of interest (again, not a shock in today's economy). After reviewing the resumes emailed to our firm, we narrowed down our list of possible choices—all of whom looked very good, at least on paper.

During one of the first rounds of interviews with a particular person, as the candidate was generating small talk in order to relax, he informed me that he had performed work similar to that done by our firm, which is always a good thing since the best predictor of future behavior is past behavior. In particular, the candidate had worked onsite, consulting on a project led very ably by two young women who hadn't been out of graduate school more than five years. When this person mentioned the nature of the work, it sounded eerily familiar to me, and I asked him the name of the consulting firm that had employed his services. The candidate shrugged his shoulders and said that he "couldn't recall" the name of the company as it was about two years ago, but that the work was interesting and clearly rather challenging.

Next, I asked our prospective candidate if he recalled the names of the two young women leading the project, but again, he failed to provide anything more specific than that they were both rather attractive, quite bright, and that one of them spoke with an Eastern European accent. Hmmm, I thought, this really does sound familiar. Then I asked if one of the two women was named Christina, and he responded in a somewhat surprised fashion that he thought it "sounded about right." Trying yet another line of attack to jog his memory, I asked this seemingly bright young man if he got paid for his work, and he responded by saying, "right away." Playing my final trick of the hand, I asked if perchance he noticed who signed his paycheck. "No, no, I don't recall," again, came the reply. You get the picture by now. I then very calmly explained—even though pretty agitated inside—that I had signed his check, and the firm which had conducted the project was mine.

At that point, the candidate inquired, "I guess this interview is over." To which I replied, "Yup, it certainly is."

The moral of the story: Do your homework!

Clearly, this example is extreme, but it should serve to illustrate that going into a job interview (if you are even lucky enough to land one), you need to prepare yourself. In the case of this candidate, he failed to perform his due diligence and was made to look silly as he had actually had a previous connection, and therefore, a natural "in" at the place where he was applying for further work.

Your New Friends: The Internet and Its Search Engines

Today, thanks to modern technology and the Internet, it is possible to learn just about anything about anybody. Taking the time to type in the name of the company where you are applying into a search engine such as Google as noted above will help you craft a cover letter that is more targeted than the generic "To whom it may concern." Likewise, prior to visiting a prospective employer for a round of job interviews, it is important you look carefully at what information exists online about the company, and quite possibly, about the people whom you will be meeting in order to be well informed and well prepared so that you can come across as a person who the organization would like to invite back for a second round of interviews.

The first step is to visit the company's Web site and learn as much as you can about the organization. The company's history, to include its primary products and services, is a good place to start. If the company has a mission statement or an explanation of its values, you need to ask, is this a place where you will feel comfortable and at home? If the company is publicly traded, it helps to know about the financial health of the organization. Did it make money during the recession, and what about during good times? What have been its trend lines for sales and profitability? Does the company have a portfolio of products or services that are unique and not easily replicated? As Warren Buffet said, "Is there a deep moat around the business," making it hard for others to replace the company's products and services once they have been purchased or installed? With that said, what companies compete against the business? Is this a business that has a viable future, or will technology overtake it, or worse, is it in a line of business, where its primary functions—to include the one to which you are applying—will be sent offshore at some point in the future? Finally, what has the business press reported about the company? Have there been any major breakthroughs? What about reported downsides like buyout rumors or recovery from a recent bankruptcy?

Besides checking on the business itself, it makes sense to use the Internet's search engines to learn more about the people whom you will be meeting. Nothing breaks the ice more effectively than connecting with somebody on a personal level or talking to them about their accomplishments. Obviously, it is best if you can connect on a job-related subject, but very often, having something in common with your interviewers such as an interest in running, dining out, fly fishing, travel, or independent films can serve as an ice breaker and a way to build instant rapport. Since people want to hire employees with whom they feel comfortable, anything you can do ahead of time to break down barriers and bridge gaps are to your advantage.

The next step is to use services like Linked-In to see if you have any connections that might know people at the company. Continue doing your homework to see if you can get some first-hand information about the company from people that might have worked there or did business with the organization. Maybe, one of your contacts will serve as a reference who can talk to people at the company ahead of time and put in a good word for you. Perhaps one of your contacts knows a person in the group scheduled to interview you.

Asking for advice on the person's style and personality can make a big difference. Many years ago, prior to approaching a prospective client about using our firm's services to evaluate new hires at his company, a colleague tipped me off about the person who would be making the final decision and stated very clearly that while this individual appreciated humor, at the same time, he did very little to initiate or exude it. Moreover, my friend cautioned me not to try to "warm him up" with my corny jokes. Doing so would only fall on deaf ears while getting me tossed out on my ear. He was absolutely right. This person had probably had a charisma bypass and not much would get him to laugh. Since I wasn't auditioning for a spot at the local comedy club, I kept it very serious and focused. It worked.

Based on your initial due diligence you can begin to think about the kinds of examples you will cite if asked for specifics about your past accomplishments. It is also a good idea to have a list of questions of your own that you can ask about the company based on what you have learned ahead of time. Even the list of references you will give can be tailored to suit the needs of the company based on who might be viewed as more credible by the hiring organization.

In conclusion, while much is made about proper etiquette in following up on job interviews with thank you notes either written by hand or sent as emails, far too little attention is given to preparing for interviews ahead of time. There is no excuse not to be well prepared ahead of time. In fact, failing to do your homework will almost always be viewed as an affront by the company as well as a sign of laziness or a lack of conscientiousness, whether deserved or not. You have the tools at your disposal. At no time in our history has there been so much ready access to information online, in the business press, and through a company's own public relations via Web sites, brochures, and other collateral PR and marketing materials.

What Should You Wear for an Interview?

Anyone who has seen me dress without the help of my wife knows that I have just about zero credibility on dressing for success. Hence, I make no attempt to broach that topic. There are plenty of other fashion gurus available for helpful advice, and I'm not one of them. Nevertheless, the question always comes up about dressing appropriately for a job interview. If the company is highly informal as are many places of work, wearing a three-piece business suit will cause you to stick out like a sore thumb and draw unnecessary attention to your appearance. On the other hand, dressing too casually when the company is more formal is probably an even worse mistake.

While the general rule of thumb is to probably over-dress as opposed to under-dress, we can offer a few more helpful hints. First, if you are familiar with someone at the company or know someone who is, you can simply ask the individual what is the standard dress code at the company. The HR department might have a set of guidelines posted online for job candidates, and this is a good place to start as well. Regardless, being neatly groomed and in proper attire counts for a lot. Earlier in the book, we talked about the false indicators of appearance and verbal skills as variables overly weighted in the final hiring decision process. While we believe they are given far too much attention at the expense of other more relevant factors, it is important to make a favorable first impression. In the event that all of the above suggestions for determining the right way to dress for your interview lead down a blind alley, you can always make a simple inquiry by email or voicemail asking about the suggested dress code for job candidates. We offer this as a solution of last resort since it is always better to obtain this information from other sources, but in the end, you do not want to look out of place and ruin your chances after you've done all of your homework.

Getting to Your Appointment on Time

Punctuality is important in any job, and being late for your interview appointment will probably do little to impress your prospective employer and will imply that you can't manage your time effectively. Still, if you have never been to the company's place of business before, you won't know how long it takes to drive to that location. Again, your old friend, the Internet, with MapQuest or other similar search engines, can provide you with a set of directions, but we want to add a few cautions. For example, the routing offered by these services might not always be the most direct. In addition, they are not always informed about major road repairs and construction work.

While it might sound like overkill or the advice of a highly obsessive-compulsive personality type (which would not be too far from the mark), we strongly suggest doing a test run if you are totally unfamiliar with the location of your interview appointment. If you are driving to your appointment, drive to the location ahead of time over the weekend or during the day if you are out of work. Better yet, try making the drive during the rush hour if you are meeting with somebody first thing in the morning. This will help you get oriented as to which routes to follow and even where to park if the location is in a large city.

For those who might consider public transportation to work, we suggest a dry-run on the train or bus so that you know where to board and where to get off for your appointment. Get a sense of the walk required after arriving at the train station or getting off at the bus stop. While all of this advice might appear over the top, remember that you are not doing yourself any favor by rushing to your appointment out of breath and disheveled from having to run a few blocks or becoming exasperated in heavy traffic. Again, punctuality is one of those deal breakers, and there's no sense having the job interview over before it starts.

Practicing Ahead of Time: Perfecting Your Elevator Speech and Using Role Plays

There is a fine line between sounding too poised as though you were acting in a play production and being too confident in the delivery of your words. Obviously, fumbling for words or sounding tongue-tied will likely hurt you. That is why it is helpful to rehearse for your interviews. Even before you actually interview with a company, it is a good idea to have your "elevator speech" down pat for such activities as networking events or any type of social gathering that might put you in contact with people who can refer your name or recommend your services to a potential employer. As most people know, the classic definition of an elevator speech is the ability to describe what you are looking for in the time it would take to ride down the elevator in a regular downtown office building. In other words, can you summarize yourself in thirty seconds or less?

This is an important part of the job search process since you will only have a few seconds to tell people enough about yourself to gain their interest and attention. Longwinded explanations or convoluted descriptions of your qualifications are a surefire way to discourage people from considering you as a credible candidate. Moreover, as will be discussed in greater detail, when we talk about job interviews, talking too much is a major killer in the hiring process. How many times have we seen viable candidates literally talk themselves out of a job? Say what you need to say and say no more. If asked to elaborate, then you can add more detail. Most people, however, deliver far too much information, or as younger people say today, "that's TMI." In sum, keep your answers succinct and to the point and don't go off on tangents.

If you are unsure how you sound or need extra help, we suggest role playing with a trusted friend or partner who might be able to give you feedback and allow you an opportunity to practice "your lines" so that you won't be self-conscious when the time comes to talk in front of other people. An inability to overcome shyness and the fear of speaking to strangers has been known to be harmful to otherwise excellent candidates. Just as in anything—sports or music—practice makes perfect. In sum, before you get in front of the people who will be making important decisions about your career, make sure you have practiced to near perfection what you will tell them and how you anticipate responding to their inquiries and comments about your qualifications. For those who struggle with shyness and stage fright we recommend turning to organizations like Toastmasters.

Come Prepared with Notes and to Take Notes

By now, you should have the idea that we propose the Boy Scout motto: "Be Prepared." This means having all of the questions you want to ask written down on a sheet of paper ahead of time. It will be important to have a list of the names of the people you will be meeting on paper as well. Moreover, make sure you know how to pronounce their names correctly. If you are unsure, ask someone at the company ahead of time, a receptionist or an administrative assistant can serve as good resources for you. If you are unsure, stand ready to be corrected. Many, many years ago, during the depths of the last Great Depression, Dale Carnegie authored his famous book, How to Win Friends and Influence People. Read it! One of his most important points is that the sweetest sound to almost anyone's ears is his or her own name. Without sounding overly familiar or ingratiating, use people's names during your interviews. A word of caution, however, be sure to address the person with respect, Mr. or Ms. is the safest approach until corrected otherwise.

One word of advice that is useful concerns the possible mispronunciation of a person's name or even using the wrong name.

Early in an encounter, people are generally forgiving when you call "Don" "Dan" or "Pat" "Pam." However, if after spending an hour with them or encountering them later in the day and for whatever reason you are still making the same mistake, people will be far less forgiving. While the point might strike the reader as petty, there is no justification in giving a person a ready-made reason to reject you, especially since the situation is so easily correctable.

Besides knowing the names of the people on your appointment list, having a set of questions that demonstrate that you've done your homework is critical. By being able to demonstrate knowledge of the company and its products and services as well as the markets served by the organization, you are signifying your preparedness along with a level of conscientiousness. Unlike our friend in the opening vignette, don't be ignorant of the organization. It will project an image that you are unprepared or lackadaisical, which will likely take you out of competition with the other applicants for the same role.

Besides having a prepared set of notes, background information, and follow-up questions, be ready to take notes during your interviews. While copying every word that is spoken to you will make you look like a first year college student in the lecture hall, it is a good idea to have a pen handy so that when an important piece of information is offered, you will be able to retain it. For example, any comments or remarks about the prevailing values and corporate culture are worth transcribing. If for no other reason, you can check for consistencies between interviewers. Are all your interviewers espousing the same philosophy? Or is there sufficient discrepancy to make you wonder about the messages the company communicates to its employees? Other important information pertains to new products or possible activities that might directly impact your employment such as talk or rumors of impending acquisitions. Remember, first in is often first out in a corporate downsizing initiative.

Finally, the act of simply taking notes when others are speaking shows respect and consideration for their thoughts and observations. It communicates a message that you are a serious candidate for the job and you wish to learn as much as possible ahead of time. Having such information at your fingertips will also be helpful when you are preparing your thank you notes and emails to the company. By properly spelling a person's name or title (be sure to ask for business cards to help you) and making reference to a point or two you discussed during your interview, you will separate yourself from the pack of people who send the standard, perfunctory thank you reply to prospective employers.

CHAPTER SEVEN

Running the Gauntlet Part I—Online Testing

Part I: Online Testing

A (Very) Brief History and Overview of Testing

Despite the high technology of online testing, employment testing itself is hardly a new field. In fact, its history and initial uses date back almost a century to the start of the First World War. (Don't worry, this will not be a recounting of one hundred years of testing's greatest hits). In short, however, testing was born out of a pressing need to select and place soldiers during the Great War. With so many new arrivals in the United States who did not speak English as their primary language, plus a number of new recruits who were not sufficiently literate, the military had to develop a program to measure people's potential, utilizing both verbal and non-verbal testing. The overwhelming success of the two newly developed tests, Army Alpha and Army Beta, set in motion a movement to apply similarly successful procedures in business and industry.

From the 1920s through the 1960s, testing grew in popularity. It became a part of the very fabric of most personnel (now human resources) departments. Most new hires were subject to some kind of aptitude testing to measure basic math and verbal skills as well as special talents for solving mechanical problems or thinking creatively. Of course, there was little concern or worry if the tests discriminated against certain groups of employees based on gender, race, or national origin. With the advent of the Civil Rights Movement, however, there were challenges to testing, and ultimately employers had to prove two things, usually after being taken to court. First, those companies that administered tests to job applicants had to show their tests were valid. This meant that there had to be a statistical relationship between high (and low) scores on the test and high (and low) performance on the job. If the test was unable to predict subsequent job performance with any degree of accuracy, it was not considered valid, and as a result, it needed to be dropped immediately. Second, test givers had to show that their testing tools did not rule out large groups of minorities or women; hence, causing unintended discrimination.

With the growing number of lawsuits being filed against companies that relied on testing to hire employees, the practice soon lost its original luster, and many companies simply decided not to test rather than face a mountain of litigation. Today, testing has seen a revival of sorts due in large part to several factors. First, there is the growth of the Internet, which allows a whole range of testing products to be hosted on various Web sites. These tests include personality inventories for online dating services, aptitude tests to determine if you're right for real estate sales or an overseas assignment, and so on and so forth. The ease of Internet-based testing makes it convenient to administer and score. Second, the number of college students pursuing careers in industrial and organizational psychology has grown dramatically. The Society for Industrial and Organization Psychology, simply known as SIOP, now boasts more members than ever before, and it's still growing. One of the core competencies of these individuals is in test design and development of sophisticated testing tools, often to be administered online. Finally, as the depth of the Great Recession beginning in 2008 has increased, there is a need to screen more cost-effectively the large number of applicants who apply for a scarcity of jobs. When taken together, these factors have resulted in a renaissance for testing.

The "Science" of Testing

As implied about testing from its earliest days nearly a century ago, there is a rigor to implement a testing program. Experimental design and statistics play a large role in designing and validating testing tools for both fairness and effectiveness. Most industrial and organizational psychologists who are involved in the process are trained in the scientific method. While psychology and all of its many branches are a social science, most testing instruments are not designed in a slipshod or haphazard fashion. The fact that such tests have predictive power based on statistical validity speaks to this point.

At the same time, an overreliance on test results at the expense of other equally or more relevant information is a mistake. In short, I have always believed that tests are never conclusive; they are merely instructive. Yet because tests involve hard numbers and their results can be placed on fancy graphs, which often compare the test taker to a wide range of norm groups, there is an even greater appearance of scientific rigor to the whole process. Of course, besides seeming to be scientific, testing, especially when administered online, is also inexpensive and easy. Companies can have people take them online conveniently in the comfort of their own homes, and the results are then automatically scored and sent back to the prospective employer so that a fast and seemingly informed decision can be made on a candidate's suitability for employment.

Unfortunately, no amount of caution that we can provide will limit the use of testing as a final decision maker so early in the hiring process. During my talks to those out of work, questions are often asked from the members of the audience about this or that particular test. With so many testing instruments on the market, it is hard to keep up with all of them. Some tests come from reputable publishing houses and are well known to professional and laypeople alike. Others are homegrown and not subject to the rigorous standards of validation mentioned above, where the testing tools must demonstrate a statistically significant relationship to predicting job success or the behavior which it purports to measure, whether it be work ethic or sales aptitude, or the ability to work cooperatively with others in teams. For the naïve job applicant, it is a challenging chore to know with some degree of confidence which tests are truly valid and developed with academic rigor and which were made up by some charlatan who claims to be an expert in predicting behavior.

What Do Tests Measure?

So what do these tests actually measure? Most tests are designed with a specific purpose in mind. As will be seen below, testing in general breaks down into two large categories: mental ability testing and personality assessment. For the time being, however, let's discuss what employers think they are getting as a result of administering some kind of testing tool. Most employers think that they are receiving an accurate picture of a person's aptitude or ability as measured by the test that is being administered. For example, if a person is taking a test to measure sales aptitude, which allegedly predicts a person's ability to survive and prosper in a profession where they are selling for a living, then the employer can enjoy a certain amount of comfort in picking people who score high on the instrument. If an employer wants to promote teamwork among the employees at the company, then a high score on a test of people skills and collaborative behavior will probably predict success for interacting with people on a frequent basis in the workplace. And so it goes.

Before a company rejects a potential job applicant, there are certain things that have to be taken into consideration. For example, does the test really measure what it claims to measure? Just because there are credible questions about selling in the face of rejection or working with all kinds of people in a diverse workforce, it does not necessarily mean that the final test score is an entirely accurate predictor. Perhaps, even more important, however, is the observation that most people fake their test results in order to look good. This is especially true in those instances when the tests do not have "right" and "wrong" answers as opposed to mental ability tests that measure math or verbal aptitude along with logical reasoning skills.

Faking, in fact, is a huge problem for the testing industry, in particular, when it comes to the use of personality questionnaires. Regardless of whether the test is administered with a proctor in reasonably controlled circumstances or online through the Internet, the test taker will want to act in his or her own best interests and "shade" their responses in order to look good or at least avoid being ruled out of the hiring process before there is an opportunity to meet a real person face to face for an interview regarding an actual job opening. While certain tests have ways or specific test scales designed to measure for social desirability, these scales are rather crude and often don't go far enough to identify faking, when a tendency exits to respond to questions in the most favorable light. As we mentioned previously, with at least five people pursuing every one job opening, who wouldn't want to give themselves an added advantage by looking exemplary? As will be discussed below, however, very little good comes from trying to make yourself appear like someone who you are not.

In summary, tests are basically shortcuts used by employers to weed out people who are unlikely to perform well on the job in the event an offer of employment was extended to them. While we can understand how companies want to save everyone time and money (especially themselves), nevertheless, relying on test results alone serves neither party very well.

Cognitive Ability Tests Versus Personality Inventories

In getting down to specifics, there are two basic types of testing tools. One measure examines cognitive capabilities and is critical to jobs that require a certain level of thinking skills in order to perform the job effectively. The other type of test, which is probably more prevalent, is the personality inventory. These instruments do not have "right" and "wrong" answers, but companies will look at them in a way that can lead to ruling in or out candidates for various employment opportunities. As noted above, because these particular testing tools are subject to faking and distortion, it is doubtful if they are really providing an accurate measure of the individual filling out the questions.

First, let's talk about mental ability testing, and let's begin with some common misconceptions about these kinds of tools. To many people, these instruments are seen as IQ tests, which measure a person's intelligence. Formal IQ testing is not something that is done online or within a twenty-minute exam. There are trained mental measurement experts, mostly in fields like school or educational psychology, who actually sit down with people for many hours, often covering the better part of the day, and test individuals on everything from vocabulary skills to memory recall for facts and figures as well as spatial aptitudes, verbal analogies, and logical reasoning skills. At the end of the day, a whole battery of these tests yields a score that is probably as close to a measure of IQ (the intelligence quotient) as can reasonably be expected given the state of our testing tools today.

In short, quickie, online math and verbal reasoning tests are not IQ tests, and it is a mistake to construe them as such. Even the more prominent mental ability tests administered to high school seniors looking to attend college like the ACT or the SAT are not pure IQ tests. In fact, what they are really designed to predict is performance in college-level courses during a person's first year at school. With that said, however, scores on these two well-regarded instruments tend to correlate positively with measures of IQ. In other words, a person who scores high on his or her ACT or SAT would be likely to score well on the more in-depth IQ tests administered by a recognized testing expert, who has been trained in mental measurement and psychometrics. Despite such warnings, there are many employers who think that they have adequately assessed a person's intelligence by using these mental ability tools.

What is probably still more important is what a mental ability test really does predict. Yes, for certain jobs, the higher the mental horsepower, the more likely the job applicant will succeed on the job. In particular, for positions in science and engineering along with certain roles in high finance or the law being very bright is a competitive advantage to both the person and the organization which hires that individual. But for most jobs, mental ability is what is sometimes called a "threshold competency." Two authors, Kolb and Boyatzis, in their book, The Competent Manager (John Wiley and Sons, 1982), first used the term "threshold competency" to explain that in many jobs, especially the ones with a relatively high level of responsibility, it is important to be smart. Yet too little or too much of this attribute (intelligence) can spell trouble. Obviously, companies want to hire people who can handle the mental complexities of the work, but if a person is "too smart," he or she will be reluctant to listen to other people's input and probably think his or her own answers are the best. Naturally, this is a recipe for disaster by eliminating collaboration and cooperation in the organization.

Today, much is made about E.Q. or emotional intelligence, which is a nice segue into personality assessment. But before we make this transition, however, let's talk about emotional intelligence. While there are books on the topic, it is a matter that is subject to much debate—and for a good reason: it is hard to define. Some people have referred to it as a measure of empathy or sensitivity to the feelings and moods of other people. For others, E.Q. is just another name for common sense of good judgment. Because it is hard to define, it will obviously be difficult to measure accurately. Of course, this has not precluded certain ambitious test developers from claiming they have a tool to measure the concept. The point is that for many complex jobs in sales, marketing, operations, supply chain, and human resources to name just a very few, relying on solely a cognitive ability test to rule in or rule out a potential job applicant is ill advised at best.

From a technical perspective, measures of personality are not really tests in the true sense of the word. More specifically, these tools cannot really be defined as "tests" since they lack "right" and "wrong" answers. While there might be a consensus from the test publisher's point of view based on "expert" input and advice about what is the best way of responding to any individual item on a personality inventory, in the end, interpreting the answers (and the questions as they are worded) is a judgment call. As noted above, these instruments or questionnaires as they are technically known are easily subject to faking and distortion. The problem for most test takers is that they are confused. For example, they are confused about what the test is actually trying to measure, confused about the best way to answer the items honestly or truthfully without ruling themselves out of a job, and finally, confused about why so much weight is placed on these tools when applicants have a whole body of work to support their candidacy for various job openings in their chosen field or profession.

Most personality tests try to classify people into broad categories generally using some clever name like "creators," "drivers," "consensus builders," or "visionaries." The tests typically cast people into one of the four personality types based on some combination of their desire to get results and their attitude about working around other people. Individuals who rank high on drive and relationship orientation are often seen as charismatic leaders. Those who are the opposite—low on drive and low on relationship-orientation—are more reserved and analytical in their approach. Moreover, people with high drive and ambivalent attitudes about cultivating relationships are often described as taskmasters or slavedrivers if you want to get nasty. Those who care a lot about other people and their feelings but are not quite as driven are seen as more amicable and friendly—often the kinds of people who collaborate effectively in a team setting.

In addition, today there are a number of personality inventories based on the notion that personality can be categorized according to five factors: extraversion, agreeableness, conscientiousness, openness, and general adjustment. The Big Five as they are often called in the trade can be further subdivided into subdimensions that measure a person's anxiousness or an individual's ability to manage time or even trust other people enough to let them carry out an assignment. Of course, each job has its own set of particular demands. So in negotiating contracts, having an agreeable person in place might not serve the company very well. For jobs with high demands for after-hours entertainment such as certain sales positions, being an extrovert is critical. Finally, working in customer service demands a person who can listen and empathize, while at the same time, not be too flexible and give in to every demand on the company.

The Perils of Cheating

Online psychological testing tools have become more advanced, especially with the introduction of sophisticated technology into the process. Additionally, most of these instruments have social desirability scales, which measure faking to some extent. Incidentally, the use of these scales to detect obvious distortions in people's answers is nothing new, and in fact, their usage dates back to paper-and-pencil tests as they were termed during the last century. Despite these attempts to uncover faking, most personality-oriented tests are still highly transparent. Test takers can generally see right through them and shade their answers in such a way as to appear more sociable or more conscientious than they actually are on a regular basis. While the point of a test's questions—especially in light of a particular job as advertised and its special demands or requirements—might seem so obvious that you can influence your responses to make yourself appear as the ideal candidate, do so at your own peril. We say this for several reasons, some of which relate to the simple ethics involved in deliberately cheating, and others pertaining to important practical considerations. Attempting to be someone you're not will ultimately do no one any good, especially you. Answering questions in a way that is untruthful is in a word, wrong. There is no question that with the pressure to find work, certain people are willing to set aside their ethics for practicalities, but in the end, it is wrong, and as we will show, it is ultimately impractical.

Just looking at the practicalities of cheating or distorting your answers, suppose you do manage to fool your potential employer and land a job for which you are not well suited, and furthermore, suppose you or your new employer realizes this within the first six to nine months of your time at the company—the result is that you either resign or are asked to leave (the euphemism for getting canned). What are you then going to do with this job on your resume? As we discussed in Chapter Five, will you omit it and use years rather than months and years on your resume format to cover your tracks? Or maybe you decide to be completely truthful and include the six-to-nine-month stint on the resume, then, what will you do during each subsequent job interview? Will you want to spend half your time during your round of interviews at each prospective employer explaining why you only stayed such a short while?

For those who choose the first option to simply delete the job from their resume, remember, with today's Internet search capabilities, your association with your past employer might surface during a routine search of your background or, perhaps, by a fluke. (This is one of those instances where the Internet is not your friend!) In the event such an occurrence transpires, you will probably be summoned to the office of the HR department at your next employer and likely be dismissed for falsifying your resume. In any event, having a short-term job on your resume, which resulted because you tried to "fake" your way in the door serves no one very well in the end. In sum, honesty is the best policy from an ethical as well as a practical point of view.

Effective Strategies for Taking Tests

Since this is not a book about how to "game" the system, what possible advice can be offered for taking tests either online or tests on paper that often serve as nothing more than barriers to entry for job candidates? This next section will focus more on realistic and helpful considerations when taking tests. Since there are two types of tests as explained above, there will be different ways to approach each type of test.

For mental ability tests, there is less use of these instruments online because of the inability to monitor or proctor against cheating. On the other hand, certain logical reasoning tests defy cheating because going to a dictionary to look up the meaning of a word or using a calculator to solve a math problem is not going to be very helpful. However, if a company is using mental ability testing of any kind and you have not taken these kinds of tests since high school or college, here are some suggestions. First, you are no doubt rusty. One of the best ways to get "back into shape" is to go to a bookstore or order online the books high school and college students use to prepare for entrance exams, like the SAT, ACT, or GRE (Graduate Record Examination). These manuals contain plenty of vocabulary and math problems as well as ones covering logic and problem solving. It has also been suggested by certain coaching experts to keep your mind active by doing crossword puzzles or other kinds of games that keep you mentally fit and alert.

However, the biggest concern I've heard from groups of unemployed individuals is not about the mental ability tests given by companies, but instead, they complain about the personality inventories and how to take them. In particular, there are two issues that emerge regarding personality testing. The first relates to the unfortunate situation where job applicants attempt to "out think" the test and end up outsmarting themselves. The second issue involves the question asked by many applicants: "Do I respond to the questions as they relate to my behavior on the job or off the job in the comfort of my own home?" Let's look at each matter individually.

As we have stated throughout the book, people want jobs, and so when they apply for a position, they will do everything in their power to appear as qualified an applicant as possible. No one, of course, can blame people for trying their hardest to gain re-employment. However, in attempting to gain an advantage, job candidates will distort their responses to questions on personality inventories in ways that actually work to their disadvantage in addition to the reasons cited previously. For example, in applying for a sales opening, many applicants are prescreened using online testing tools. In trying to outwit the test, candidates will attempt to appear outgoing and extroverted, when in fact, this is not an accurate picture of their inclinations. By making themselves appear more social than what is comfortable for them, applicants inadvertently might harm their candidacy. By way of further explanation, in certain sales roles, being too outgoing and social is a disadvantage because the job might actually call for long periods of isolation or alone time. For example, certain outside sales positions might require a lot of travel. This could mean long periods of time on the road traveling from account to account. In addition, high travel jobs demand nights away from home staying at motels along the way. For the person with high needs to talk and interact with others on a frequent or regular basis, the job would likely prove a hardship. Hence, shaping your test responses to make yourself look like the "belle of the ball" will take you right out of consideration for a job opening. On the other hand, if you responded truthfully and portrayed yourself as more introverted and able to occupy your time when others aren't readily available to entertain you, it might have advanced you to the next round in the hiring process—typically, an opportunity for a job interview.

The next question that frequently arises when I speak to large groups of job seekers relates to the frame of mind one adopts when responding to questions about likes, dislikes, and other preferences along with how one behaves in various social situations. Questions about taking charge in situations or liking to be included in certain activities are examples. Also, questions about how one prefers to spend one's time are also very common. Now, in many instances, our behavior at home and at work is consistent. On the other hand, there are significant differences in the two types of behavior for many people. For example, at work, many individuals might enjoy interacting with a wide variety of people, to include going to lunch or participating in large meetings or group gatherings. Meanwhile, once settled into the comfort of one's home, reading a good book or spending time alone on a special hobby might just be what the doctor ordered, so to speak.

In other instances, people might be highly disciplined and organized in their work routines, writing detailed "To Do" lists or using their Outlook or Lotus Notes calendar functions to schedule every available minute. At home, however, a person might prefer an element of spontaneity, where activities are not so rigidly structured and planned. Being able to go with the flow is much preferred to a datebook, with every minute accounted for during after-hours or weekends. Likewise, questions about taking orders to being in-charge might reflect situations that vary greatly between home and office. Being king of the castle at home might be a luxury that cannot be afforded on the job. Or for many of us, it's quite the other way around. Being the office tyrant is not allowed in the house (according to my spouse, the ruler of the roost at home), and we must become the serfs and subjects that our spouses prefer and expect.

Thus, the critical question of how to respond to open-ended and ambiguous questions about one's behavior and preferences is simple. Respond as you would when considering your behavior at the office and not at home. Clearly, there is a critical difference in some instances. While we might like to paddle around the house in our jammies and slippers, looking sharp and ready to meet with the most sophisticated customers and clients is what is called for at the office. Other behaviors (which shall go unnamed) might be acceptable in the comfort of one's own home, but again, forbidden with good reason in the workplace. While people don't exactly have split personalities between the two venues, there is a significant difference and responding to questionnaire items in the context of the workplace is by far the safest bet.

Finally, just a word or two about answering items that call for you to respond on some type of scale that goes from one extreme to another—in particular, scales that are anchored by responses that state "strongly agree" or "strongly disagree." There is absolutely nothing wrong or potentially harmful in responding to either alternative if that is how you really feel about a matter. On the other hand, think about the question for a minute, and before making a choice, ask yourself: "Do I really feel that strongly one way or another about the item?" If the test question elicits a strong reaction on your part, by all means answer accordingly. On the other hand, if the item really isn't something you care about a great deal, respond in a more moderated fashion. In short, try to avoid the extremes. The reason is simple, most personality testing tools are designed to measure your reactions to a wide array of subjects. The more extreme you look or try to make yourself appear, the more you will put yourself in a box that you likely don't intend.

Many people today speak of their "passion" for certain things. From our perspective, the term is far too frequently misused, and it tends to dilute the impact of the true meaning of the word. Case in point, as our son approached his senior year in college, he was applying for various jobs in the business world. One opportunity was particularly attractive for him, and he wrote to the owner of the business that he had a "passion for real estate." He then asked me to review his cover letter and resume, when my eye caught the overused and misapplied term "passion." Rather perplexed, I asked him if he was really so "passionate" about real estate. He persisted with a "yes." Then I asked him if his feelings for real estate were equal to how he felt about one especially pretty coed he dated during his junior year. More specifically, I candidly asked him if the feelings he had while on a date with this girl were the same feelings he had for real estate, and if they were both the same, then he certainly could include the term "passion for real estate" in his cover letter to the company. You guessed it, we never heard about his passion for real estate ever again, and yes, he did get the job, and he likes it very much.

CHAPTER EIGHT

Running the Gauntlet Part II—Interviewing

Vignette: The Candidate Who Talked Too Much

If your resume has caught the eyes of the right people and you've survived the online testing process, it is now time to move onto the next step: the job interview. For many people, reaching this round in the hiring process is an achievement in itself, especially in today's snake-bit economy. How many times have you read in the newspapers or heard on television or over the Internet about the job seeker who sent out hundreds of resumes and didn't receive so much as a call back? After you put so much effort and hard work to finally land an interview, now consider the case of the candidate who simply talked too much.

On paper our ideal candidate looked terrific. He had many years of manufacturing experience, and in particular, he had spent nearly twenty-five years working in our client's highly unique industry, which required a firm knowledge of operations management along with expertise in building the kind of products manufactured at our client's large plant facility located in the Midwest.

To add to the allure of this applicant, our firm tested this person and found that he possessed unusually high mental ability and cognitive capacity based on a test of logical reasoning and analytical thinking skills. This was especially impressive since the candidate had only completed a couple of years in college prior to leaving school to get married, and yet, he scored in the range normally seen with job applicants who not only had bachelor's degrees, but in many cases, these same high-testing individuals also have gone on to graduate school to complete their MBA degrees.

So what happened to our perfect candidate for my client's General Manager job? He talked too much. Beginning with the simple question about how many years he had been in manufacturing, the candidate began with his first job as a laborer at a factory in high school, and before I could get a word in edgewise to slow him down and just give me the total number of years, he had worked his way right through to his most recent role. More than twenty-five years of history were provided along with almost twenty minutes of wasted time before we could move on to the next question. Offering more information than was either required, or quite frankly, requested by me, our candidate was setting the tone for a failed interview, and a golden opportunity was fumbled away.

I listened to this person tell a supporting story for each and every point he made. For example, when asked what he liked and disliked about his work over the years, the candidate felt compelled to provide a lengthy and tedious account to show why each aspect of his list of likes and dislikes was either so enjoyable or so dissatisfying. Again, a simple listing of the most satisfying and least satisfying aspects of his work would have sufficed and been much appreciated as well. When we finally did get down to asking him questions that required more in-depth and detailed answers in order to understand how he dealt with various scenarios such as start-up operations and turnaround situations, little time was left for our applicant to make his case for why he was the best qualified candidate for the General Manager job.

Naturally, our candidate stated that his strongest attributes were his focus and efficiency. While it is true he probably did practice "MBWA" (management-by-walking-around), we can only imagine how much time he consumed walking (and talking) from one end of the plant floor to the other. It was also not surprising that this same individual described his greatest skill as a leader as being a "coach." All too often, we have found in our assessment practice that people who like to talk and even lecture others view themselves as great coaches. In short, verbosity and perceived coaching skills are closely related. One can only imagine (and pity) his captive audience of direct reports and plant employees who had to sit and listen to our person's gratuitous advice for hours on end. Finally, knowing that our applicant would be reporting to a company CEO who was all-business and no-nonsense in wanting to just get the facts and nothing but the facts, the match between the two would be a disaster.

The bottom line: after so many months of sending out countless resumes and trying to arrange an interview, when the opportunity finally arose, our applicant, who looked so promising on paper, dropped the ball. Our client politely but firmly told him that he was no longer a candidate in the hiring process. Sad but true—this individual had literally talked himself out of a job.

Telephone Interviews

In today's busy world of business, the notion of doing things faster and more efficiently makes telephone interviewing an attractive tool to help screen candidates for job openings. The individuals conducting telephone screening interviews can include in-house human resources staff, typically members of the HR department's recruiting staff. Outside recruiting services and even industrial/organizational psychologists such as the individuals employed in my firm can also conduct these kinds of interviews. The questions are typically straightforward and designed to determine if you would be an appropriate candidate for the job under consideration. While final decisions about extending a job offer are rarely made as a result of these interviews, they can be the basis for early elimination in the hiring process. So be ready and alert to perform at your best.

Typically, such encounters take from thirty or forty-five minutes to an hour; some have been known to run longer. But since efficiency is the operative term, most telephone interviews will be shorter versus longer in length. In light of this observation, we would strongly suggest that the applicant be aware of the time limit he or she is facing by simply asking the interviewer at the beginning of the conversation about how much time will be required to conduct the interview. On many occasions, the interviewer will set the "ground rules" at the start of the conversation by saying exactly how much time will be needed to conduct the interview session. Generally, shorter interviews are used as a cursory screening tool that, if navigated successfully by the candidate, will likely lead to a next round of interviews. Regardless of the time allotted to the interview, especially if between forty-five minutes and an hour, it is important to answer all questions directly and avoid talking too much.

Although the so-called nuances of "body language" are missing, unless the interviewer uses Skype or some form of teleconferencing technique, the whole notion of making important judgments about a candidate's posture and eye contact is vastly overrated. Moreover, the idea of focusing exclusively on a candidate's capabilities as opposed to being distracted by appearance makes a lot of sense. At the same time, certain jobs as we mentioned previously in this book require a strong positive impact as generated by personal appearance. For example, certain sales roles where the candidate will only have a few minutes in front of a prospective customer could fall under this heading.

In participating successfully in a telephone interview so that you can advance to the next round, it is important to consider the following points. First, if possible, try to initiate or take the call on a landline as opposed to a cellular telephone. Now, in today's cost-conscious environment many people—especially those who are younger (and more hip)—only have a cell phone and not a landline. If you are one of these modern individuals, make sure you check with the interviewer to determine if that person is able to hear you clearly. Dropped calls during a phone interview do not bode well for advancing further in the interview process. Similarly, make sure your surroundings are quiet and free of distraction. Barking dogs, screaming children, and television sets blaring in the background all obviously detract from projecting a professional image. Even in those instances where you will not be seen by a teleconferencing tool, be sure to dress comfortably and sit up straight in order to pay maximum attention to the person on the other end of the line. Slouching in your chair or talking with feet up on the desk encourages a casual attitude that is also likely to be reflected in your tone of voice.

Besides positioning yourself to pay attention and stay focused, we have a few other helpful suggestions for maximizing your time on the telephone with the interviewer. Many times, telephone interviews are used to verify the information on your resume and to add a little color to the experiences you have listed on that document. Therefore, it is a good idea to have a copy of your resume handy as you speak to the interviewer. Similarly, it is a good idea to have information at your fingertips from performance appraisals and even 360-degree feedback surveys if they have been conducted on you by your peers and staff members as well as your bosses. While the information in some of these documents might cite potential limitations, being forthright and honest will win you more points than trying to conceal such findings only to have them revealed later in the process, either through reference checks or the observations of the team of people who will interview you in greater depth at your potential place of work.

In addition to having the proper documentation at your fingertips, you will want to have notes readily available to discuss the highlights and setbacks we will discuss later in this chapter. While reading from these materials will create a "canned" or overly prepped impression which the interviewer will sense right away, you don't want to be fumbling for information to support your responses so that you sound unprepared and caught off guard. In general, it is better to be overprepared than underprepared, but with that statement in mind, it is also important to understand that not all of the information you have prepared will require use during your telephone interview. In fact, the attempt to utilize all the information you have at your disposal will result in an information dump of sorts that will cause you to talk too much and likely disqualify yourself as an applicant in the early rounds of the hiring process. Also remember that even though this might be your first opportunity to talk to a "live voice" about a job opening, the person on the other end of the telephone probably speaks to dozens of candidates each day. So be considerate of that person and do not overcommunicate and dump repetitive or irrelevant information on him or her.

Once again, listen carefully to what is asked of you and only answer the question being posed to you and avoid going off on tangents. This is why it is so important that you situate yourself in a setting where you can devote total concentration to the interviewer's questions and line of inquiry. On the occasions of both telephone and face-to-face interviews, where the candidate has lost his or her sense of perspective and overanswered the question, there is a common thread or theme to the situation. In particular, most candidates tend to become too chatty when they are trying to defend themselves or rationalize an aspect of their past behavior, which they feel might reflect poorly on their candidacy for the job opening under consideration. For example, applicants without a college diploma often talk at (too much) length as to what caused them to leave school without finishing their degree studies. In other instances, applicants ramble on at length to rationalize why they stayed only a short while at a specific job when the rest of their resume is a picture of employment stability. Finally, defending a critical comment from a performance appraisal or the results of a 360-degree feedback survey all add time to the interview and ultimately do very little to enhance your attractiveness as an applicant. As will be seen later in this chapter, the greatest weakness you bring to any new employer is likely the greatest strength you will offer as well. Surprised? More about that shortly.

In closing, many of the principles of an effective telephone interview pertain to face-to-face interviews as well, and thus, the former technique should not be taken lightly or approached in anything less than a serious manner.

Face-to-Face Interviews

As just noted, many of the same principles pertaining to face-to-face interviews are no different than what we discussed with respect to interviews conducted over the telephone. The major difference, however, is that your appearance and first impression will be counted more heavily since your interviewer can see you as well as hear more clearly the sound of your voice. Being prompt and alert are obviously important but so is the way you introduce yourself to the people who greet you. While this might seem like a minor point, in our firm, we place a lot of weight on how people treat our administrative and support staff. If they are snippy, demanding, or arrogant, this says a lot. Moreover, if the candidate's behavior suddenly changes to a more pleasant and personable disposition in the presence of the interviewer (a professional psychologist), then this says even more about the person—and quite frankly, it's not saying a lot of good things either!

The proper attire for an interview has become a frequent topic for discussion as the range of variation in dress has increased between those organizations that are exceptionally laid-back—down to the flip-flops worn by many of the employees on any given day of the week to the companies that still maintain a formal dress code, to include suits and ties, while at the same time, allowing few, if any, casual days. The best approach as always is to play it safe. Specifically, as we noted in an earlier chapter, this means asking ahead of time, or better yet, looking on the company's website under their job postings to see if any information is provided on the best way to dress for an interview. If that proves unproductive, try contacting someone you know who works at the company or might know a person employed with the organization in order to seek their advice. All else failing: dress-up, not down. For example, at a place of business which might tolerate casual clothing, wear business casual (slacks and a dress shirt). If in doubt, wear nice clothes, suits, sport coats, and fashionably tailored business suits for women. Certainly anything that might detract from your professionalism such as flashy or revealing clothing, excessive jewelry, or heavily scented cologne or perfume will all result in leaving a lasting impression—just not the one you were hoping to create.

Arrive early. Mapquesting your route and practicing ahead of time was suggested earlier and is worth repeating. While there is no sure rule of thumb, arriving ten to fifteen minutes ahead of schedule is about right. If you have to wait, even beyond the time of your scheduled appointment, don't fret or act agitated. Use your time wisely and review company literature (for the second or third time). Looking at brochures or annual reports about the organization is a good use of your time. Don't be pretentious and whip out a copy of the Harvard Business Review from your briefcase just to impress your interviewer when he or she comes out to greet you. Because you won't have the luxury of sitting at home with written notes in front of you such as during a telephone interview, you might want to review last-minute materials you might need to recall during your interview discussion. Finally, don't talk on your cell phone or text other people. This kind of behavior—rightfully or wrongfully so—contributes to the impression that you have better things to do with your time than go on an interview to talk to a prospective employer.

While advice on offering a firm handshake might seem like a non starter, you would be surprised by the number of candidates who squeeze their interviewer's hand with the seeming intention of sending the latter person for X-rays at the nearest hospital's emergency room. In short, avoid the bonecrusher. You are not interviewing for the U.S. Olympic Wrestling Team. Similarly, men, please don't offer women a fish shake because you think they are too dainty. Extend your hand and shake firmly, and of course, look the other person in the eye and don't look the other way in the process. Enough said on the basics.

As mentioned previously, it will be important that you come to your interview appointment well prepared. This means knowing what you are going to say when asked certain standard interview questions, while at the same time, not coming off as though you have been rehearsing for a role in a school play. This means committing more to memory, and possibly role playing, with a trusted friend or family members so you feel confident about how you will be conducting yourself when the time comes to be on center stage. And finally, as we have emphasized so strongly as a theme when it comes to being interviewed for a job: listen carefully.

As your interview draws to a close, don't ask for feedback from the interviewer on how well you did; you will know soon enough as you try to continue through the hiring procedure toward your ultimate objective of finding a suitable job. Clearly, candidates are interested in getting feedback on their performance in the interview process. Many people feel that learning about how they are perceived by others will help them with future interviews. In the event that a person is not hired, or even if they are hired by the company, it might be appropriate then to ask for feedback but not before. First and foremost, it puts the interviewer on the spot. It can make a person feel uncomfortable, especially if they are on the fence about your candidacy. Second, it can place the interviewer in a tough position in that he or she might feel very favorably disposed toward you, but in the event that you are rejected for the position, they could feel at odds with those who made the ultimate hiring decision. The situation can be further exacerbated if you as a candidate raise a ruckus with the company, claiming that a particular interviewer liked you, and therefore, you demand to know why you weren't selected for the job. Finally, for the shy or more reserved interviewer, you will come across as overly assertive and probably too pushy as well.

One very important related point: please don't ask for an endorsement from the interviewer. We have heard this request far too many times. It sounds too forceful, and again, the more reticent interviewer will probably be taken aback and feel put on the spot. We suspect that this question or request for an endorsement originated with sales candidates, since this is the group that tends to pose it the most. Moreover, we think that certain people have probably advised applicants for sales positions many years ago to make such a request as verifiable proof that the candidate is capable of "asking for the order" or "closing" the sale. For all of the reasons stated above with respect to seeking feedback on your interview performance, we would suggest dropping the request. In fact, if you are a "closer," it will be readily apparent in your sales record, to include the number of times you have either met or exceeded your selling quota.

To conclude the interview, it is very appropriate to ask if there are any areas that require more information or further clarification on your part. In asking this question, pause and take your time in order to allow the interviewer to think. Don't just ask it in a perfunctory fashion and then jump up to end the interview and leave. Very often, a closing point will make a big difference. Remember, memory operates on the twin effects of primacy and recency, which means we tend to remember best what occurred at the beginning of an interaction and at the end of that same meeting. Thus, it is so important to not only make a positive first impression, but also to leave the interview setting with all parties feeling satisfied. And by clarifying any possible misunderstandings, you will help ensure that the interview closes on a high note.

Mirroring the Energy Level of Your Interviewer

While the notion of opposites attracting makes for wonderful romance, especially in the movies, in real life opposites often repel. With this in mind, it is important to make sure that the other person—in this case the interviewer—feels comfortable and relaxed. If you're anxious or nervous, it will be contagious and will adversely impact you and the interviewer's ability to perform at the best of your abilities. However, even if you are relaxed, mirroring the other person to some degree puts the two of you in sync with one another. This is an important point, but if overplayed, it can be damaging to your chances of receiving a favorable review in the interview process.

When I talk about "mirroring" your interviewer, I am referring to matching that person's energy level and style in order to operate at a consistent pace so that your interviewer feels comfortable and relaxed with you. For example, if your interviewer is low key and takes his or her time asking questions, make sure that you slow down. Don't interrupt, or worse, feel a compulsion to fill the probable silences that will occur in the interview session with idle chatter. In short, don't try to rush the person. Similarly, if your interviewer is animated and alert, pick up the pace. Make sure you maintain good eye contact and provide responses to that person's questions in a reasonably rapid fashion without coming across as manic yourself.

There is probably one real exception to this rule, and that occurs in the case when the interviewer wants to do all of the talking. This is, of course, a very poor way to conduct an interview, especially when it is so important to learn as much about the prospective applicant as possible. This, however, doesn't stop the longwinded interviewer from dominating the discussion. In the (unfortunate) event that you find yourself in the same room with such a person, here is some sagely advice—let them keep talking. While it is true that the interviewer will learn virtually nothing about you or your capabilities and that same person will rob you of an opportunity to make the case for your candidacy, in the end, things will probably work out well for you. Despite all the preparations that you made to answer the difficult questions we will discuss in a few minutes, letting the other party ramble on is really in your best interests.

At the end of the day, doing well during an interview has as much to do about how the interviewer feels about himself or herself as it does about how they feel about you. That's right. If you allow the interviewer to do all of the talking and brag about various real or imagined accomplishments, that person will leave the interview setting feeling great, and those positive feelings will then be attributed to you, even though you may not have had a chance to get a word in edgewise.

Related to this last point are the feelings you transmit to your interviewer. For example, if you are a competitive or confrontational person, and you caused the interviewer's competitive or argumentative side to arise, this is not a good thing. Similarly, if you are an affirming and optimistic person, your interviewer will likely feel positive and upbeat as a result of your interaction. This advice is not to recommend manipulating the other person—which will be readily transparent to everyone involved—instead, it involves practical guidance and suggestions on how to make sure that you don't inadvertently hurt your chances as a qualified candidate for landing a job.

Offering Specifics and Definitions to
Provide Clarity and Credibility

When conducting formal training classes for people on how to interview more effectively in order to select the best possible people for hire, I frequently ask participants to define several terms in their own words, such as "challenge," "variety," "security," "corporate politics," "micromanagement," and "paperwork." The reason for this exercise is simple: most applicants list one or more of these things as reasons for either liking or disliking their past and present employers. While the terms are used relatively frequently, a problem arises, however, because for almost each and every candidate, there is a different and distinct definition of each term.

For example, "variety" might mean having a lot of different tasks to perform each day. For others, it could mean being able to operate outdoors in the field. Similarly, "security" might mean having a steady paycheck without worrying if you will be paid from one week to the next. At the same time, some people think of security as knowing exactly what will be expected each day without having to worry about subjective and arbitrary ways of measuring one's performance and contribution to the company. For "politics," this term can mean anything from having separate silos or fiefdoms within an organization that inhibit collaboration and mutual problem solving, while for others, it could mean playing favorites or having the CEO's son-in-law run the marketing department. Finally, with respect to "micromanagement," a frequently heard complaint, it can mean being called three times a day by your supervisor to having to write a brief, one-page quarterly report on your activities.

For the reader, you too probably have your own notion of what each of these terms mean to you. Therefore, it is in your best interests to provide specificity during an interview. There is, of course, a fine line between providing so much detail and specificity that you wind up doing what we just warned against in our earlier vignette: talking too much and offering too much information. Nonetheless, by defining your terms (in twenty-five words or less) and providing examples and specifics to support your statements and answers, you will enhance your credibility with your interviewer(s). On those occasions where you are unsure of a definite answer, be honest and say so. For instance, you might not be sure where you want to be ten years from now for a whole lot of reasons from possible career options to family concerns.

One final caution for candidates is to avoid the use of buzzwords or jargon, which while familiar to you, might not be so familiar to your audience. Even when interviewing with people who are in your same field or profession such as IT (information technology) or supply chain management and logistics, using acronyms or terminology unique to that line of work can be hazardous. While in the Army, I once read a field manual that said, "a good vocabulary is better for catching than pitching." The same notion applies here to industry-specific jargon. If you hear a term or acronym used by your interviewer that others might not understand but you are able to comprehend, the better for you. Just don't go throwing these terms around without consideration for your listener.

Preparing to Discuss Your Highlights and Setbacks

Almost every kind of job interview will include questions about which achievements are the highlights of your career, along with possible inquiries about your particular setbacks and disappointments. The reasons are obvious: the best predictor of future success is based on past accomplishments. Moreover, how people have handled defeats and disappointments is also instructive in terms of providing important information about how you have coped with previous failures and what it says about your resiliency and ability to recover from prior setbacks. Since these questions are standard to most employment interviews, it is a good idea to be prepared and have ready answers at your fingertips. This way, you are not fumbling around for a response. While you don't want to come off as coached or having rehearsed your responses over and over again, forewarned is forearmed, and it is in your best interests to be primed to answer these questions.

The key to giving good answers to these kinds of questions is to prepare properly for them. First, pick out three examples of each type of situation. Think of three triumphs, and if possible, three disappointments. For each situation, be able to describe succinctly what happened. Don't provide a lot of unnecessary or extraneous details that will confuse your listener while adding little to the story. Next, be able to explain for each example why it was so important in your career. In the case of your accomplishments, cite hard data if possible like dollars saved or revenues generated. Also, it is a good idea to credit other people, where appropriate, without digressing too much from the topic at hand. Even though you are being asked about your achievement, a barrage of "I" statements can make you look conceited and self-centered.

In the case of a setback, make it significant without being melodramatic. For example, discussing a missed sale is not terribly earth shattering, however, if you were working on landing a particularly large account for months and it failed to come through, then that might be another matter.

Besides describing these examples of success and failure, be prepared to add two additional points which will enhance your credibility as a candidate. First, explain what you learned from each situation. What lessons did you take away and why have they been instructive over the course of your career? Next, be prepared to explain how you've taken those same lessons of experience and applied them going forward in your career. Adding this kind of supplemental information to these standard questions will go a long way toward making you stand out as a viable applicant for the job.

Moreover, citing lessons learned from a particular setback will enable you to show how you turned lemons into lemonade. For example, if you were terminated from a job for whatever reason, what did you learn? Did it teach you to communicate more frequently or more effectively with your boss and learn the important lessons of managing upward? Did it teach you to perform your due diligence before reaching for the proverbial brass ring? Being able to show how you have used those hard-learned lessons to successfully manage your career in other instances makes a bad experience all that much more valuable.

It has been our experience that when we have asked candidates about their highlights and setbacks, they often attribute all of their successes to themselves, while their setbacks have resulted from things beyond their control. A couple of points here. First, attributing success solely to your efforts sends a message, and it is not a very good one.

In discussing your past accomplishments as we noted above, be sure to credit other people for their efforts in helping you achieve your successes. No one likes a thunder stealer. In those instances where you encountered setbacks and disappointments, don't look to others as the cause of your misery. In this case, no one wants to hire people who are perennial victims. Think hard about your own role in your setback, and again, make sure you can explain how you've worked hard to avoid this kind of situation in the future. Remember, those who fail to learn from their past mistakes for whatever reason are doomed to repeat those mistakes.

By having several examples of successes and setbacks at your disposal, you can choose the one or two best examples to suit the interview situation in which you find yourself. One helpful hint: most organizations stress the importance of service. This not only means servicing the external customer if you are in sales or marketing as well as supply chain and operations, but in many instances, it refers to staff people in IT, HR, accounting, the law department, etc. These staff functions serve their internal customer within the organization. Therefore, also having an example of a time you went above and beyond to deliver outstanding service to your external or internal customer is something you might want to discuss if asked about it.

Behaviorial-based Interviewing

While interviews are by far the most effective way to get to know a candidate, they are subject to abuse. For example, while most organizations rely on structured interviews with each person asking a consistent set of questions, this is not always the case. Instead, interviews can digress into topics wholly unrelated to the job itself. For example, the weather, current events, or the local sports teams can dominate a discussion. Occasionally an interviewer goes off on a tangent and tells more about himself or herself as opposed to learning about the applicant. Worse, interviewers have been known to wander intentionally and unintentionally into private matters (and potentially illegal areas), which are not the province of the company, like marital status or highly personal, family-related matters.

To guard against such transgressions, as happens so frequently in our society, we overcorrect. The answer to these occasionally intrusive violations of individual rights along with preventing the raising of random subjects and dominating the discussion is a relatively new technique in the form of behaviorial-based interviewing. While one or two behaviorial-based questions are helpful and appropriate, an entire interview of them is overkill in my book.

But first, let's explain the concept. A behaviorial-based interview consists of questions like, "Tell me about a time you led a project team or task force" or "Describe the most difficult boss you ever worked for and why this person was so difficult." Other examples would be, "Tell me about a time you had to deal with an uncooperative team member and how did you handle it." The earlier example of an inquiry about delivering outstanding service is a type of behaviorial-based interview question as well.

As noted, there is nothing wrong with a few of these kinds of questions, but an entire interview can cause you to narrow your scope of answers to a single job experience. For example, we once worked with a company that had involvement in marketing a popular consumer product sold during major sporting events like the Super Bowl, NASCAR, and the NCAA Final Four. If a candidate had been assigned to a company marketing team at one of these events, we noticed that very soon all of that person's responses to their behaviorial-based interview questions were focused on this specific activity. While learning about their experience with the Super Bowl held in Miami or the Final Four in Seattle was very interesting, it was at the same time limiting, and it hurt the candidate's ability to provide us with a broader scope of his or her past expertise and experience.

Therefore, to guard against this kind of a situation from occurring, we offer a few helpful suggestions. First, go online and download a representative list of behaviorial-based interview questions. There are numerous Web sites that contain sample lists of these kinds of questions. Next, determine how you would answer these questions if they were posed to you to represent and explain examples of your behavior based on a wide range of different employers along with varied settings and situations so that you don't just talk to death about a single job or one specific employment experience.

Without doing your homework and practicing for these kinds of questions, you might find yourself caught offguard and limited in terms of how you present yourself during the course of the interview. This would be unfortunate, but it is, nevertheless, a natural outcome from this commonly accepted approach to employment interviewing. Just like any situation where you will be on center stage, be prepared and practice your presentation, while at the same time, make sure you are able to act natural and sound spontaneous.

The Mother of All Interview Questions: What is your biggest weakness?

Of course, I have saved the best for last when it comes to tough interview questions. Almost every candidate lives in fear of the mother of all interview inquiries: "What is your biggest weakness?" All too often, applicants, in order to preserve their hope of getting the job or advancing to the next round of employment interviews, offer the most ridiculous responses. I've heard people say that they "could be better spellers." Ever heard of a Spellchecker? Or what about the all-too-often heard laugher, "I work too hard." My answer to that silly-sounding response is, "I'm a boss, and I love my people who work too hard. Why would any manager be critical of you for this?" The ways that people then try to justify their answer to this most difficult of interview questions only serve to complicate an awkward situation.

Pity the poor applicant caught offguard by this question with no ready response. As we noted earlier in this chapter, there is a simple and obvious answer that applies to almost all of us. It is that our greatest strength is also likely our biggest weakness. What am I saying? Have you ever known people who are so bright that they believe they possess all the right answers? These individuals rarely consult with others or collaborate on decision making; instead, they think that their approach is always the correct one. How about the interpersonally gifted individuals who can get along with everyone and can establish rapport in an instance? These very same people often need to please everyone all of the time, and as a result, they are guilty of telling people exactly what they want to hear instead of being honest and direct. In short, their major failing is that they are people pleasers. Furthermore, what about honest and direct individuals gifted with high integrity? Can't they occasionally be given to bluntness and a lack of tact and diplomacy? The highly analytical person who can see situations from all angles is often reluctant to make a final decision, weighing each piece of evidence in an obsessively compulsive fashion, hence, suffering from indecisiveness.

You get the point. There is a not a single strength, when taken to the extreme or overextended in some way, that cannot have a downside. So acknowledging your strengths as a potential and observed weakness on occasion is the best and most honest way to answer the question. There are career coaches who will tell you to offer examples of ways you have acted to address your weaknesses, but we suggest simply being straightforward and sincere in accepting the fact that like everything else in life, you have to take the good with the bad. Finally, by owning up to your shortcomings and not trying to rationalize ways for how you overcome them, you are demonstrating real accountability and maturity.

In those instances where candidates are trying to manage their impression too carefully during a job interview, they come across as phony. This is even worse in the case of discussing one's potential shortcomings and weaknesses. As a result, potential employers will be able to read this kind of behavior rather easily. In closing, be prepared, be honest, and try to stay as relaxed as possible so that you can be yourself. Remember, you've been successful in the past, and you will succeed in the future in the right job with the right organization.

CHAPTER NINE

A Quick Word About References

Vignette: The Cocky Student—Know What They're Going to Say

Prior to attending graduate school, I was working for a well-known, but decidedly direct, and well . . . rather blunt, senior professor in psychology. This person's reputation was known far and wide as an outstanding and brilliant researcher and scholar, while at the same time, he was a classic curmudgeon. Having an opportunity to work for him was both a privilege and a pain. Overall, however, it entailed a lot more of the former than the latter. There were many lessons I learned from this person: some related to scholarship and others pertaining to life in general. The following example is one of the life lessons he passed on to me—for better or worse.

Sitting in the professor's sunny office one day at my work station, tucked away in the confines of his gigantic, academic lair, I had my back to him. Suddenly, one of my peers, a fellow student, strolled into the professor's office with a special request. In short, the student asked this professor to write a series of letters of recommendations for him so that he could continue his career at the next level. Referring to the professor by his first name was probably his first mistake rather than using the august title of "Dr." Nevertheless, the professor nodded his assent, and he said that he would indeed be willing to author a set of recommendation letters. The student politely thanked the professor, again using the latter's first name, and then calmly walked out of the room.

For my part, I was deep in thought trying to make heads or tails of the mass of data printed out on (remember) green bar paper, so I wasn't listening very well. Communicating in his normally warm and gracious manner, the old curmudgeon rapped his knuckles on his desk to get my undivided attention. Naturally, I popped my head up and asked what he wanted. Looking at me over his half moon glasses, he said, "Did you hear that?" "What?" I responded. Continuing, I said that it seemed that Rich just walked in and asked you for some letters of recommendation. I always felt the less conversation between the two of us the better (as you will soon see). "Well," he continued, "Rich asked me for my recommendation, but he didn't ask me what I would write." Even I knew this meant trouble.

Needless to say, a tearful Rich appeared at the professor's office six weeks later. Barely able to compose himself and hold back the waterworks, he demanded to know, "What did you say about me? I was rejected at all the places I applied where you wrote letters of recommendation. When I inquired about not being accepted, the voices on the other end of the phone all stated that my references letters were not very encouraging." At that point, I was looking for the hole in the floor to crawl into to avoid being part of this lively, yet embarrassing little exchange. When he was finally ready to respond, the professor was quick and to the point with his words. He said, "Rich, you're a very mediocre student who has managed to achieve surprisingly high grades at this school by glad-handing and brown-nosing most of your professors. But not me." (No kidding). If this wasn't enough inflicted pain, the professor then went on to say that he had rather modest expectations for Rich in terms of contributing to the field, and as a result of this assessment, he (professor positive, that is) thought it would be "a waste" to let Rich take a spot that might otherwise go to a more "promising and deserving" individual.

Enough said. Two weeks later, as I gathered my letters of recommendation for distribution among the members of the faculty,

I carefully asked each person—to include professor blunt—if they had any reservations about providing me with a (positive) reference. None did, and while our friend said nice things, he also informed me that I was "wasting my life" by not pursuing a career in academia. Since I've always believed in Henry Kissinger's famous maxim when he left the Harvard faculty to work in the Nixon administration that the "politics in academia are so vicious because the stakes are so small," I never looked back and regretted my decision to enter the world of business.

Vet Your References Ahead of Time

While the above little story might sound extreme, it is instructive. In short, know what your references will likely say, and be sure they will vouch for your performance. Earlier, we discouraged you as an applicant from pressing an interviewer for feedback on your performance in the interview, or worse, an endorsement of your candidacy. The reasons are obvious. These interviewers are in all likelihood meeting you for the first time, and putting them on the spot for immediate feedback one way or another is uncomfortable for them and will probably not serve your cause very well. On the other hand, your references—in order to be considered credible—should have had sufficient contact with you in order to speak intelligently about the quality of your work.

With that said, as you make a list of potential references, consider who might be in the best position to speak for your work. While your best friend at work might say glowing things about you, he or she probably doesn't have the perspective that your supervisor would be able to provide with respect to your recommendation. To prevent the embarrassment of the above-mentioned vignette, be sure to ask your references how they feel about characterizing your performance. It is also fair game to ask that individual if he or she would feel comfortable in endorsing you to another employer. If so, then you might want to ask what the person might cite. Although you don't want to put words in your reference's mouth, these are appropriate questions to ask, since a good recommendation from a well-regarded source might make the difference between a job offer or a letter (email) of rejection.

In returning to our story about the student who forgot to inquire about the professor's reference, there is another wrinkle to the story that also might be instructive. This particular professor was extremely well regarded in academic circles, both nationally and internationally, despite his winning personality. Moreover, because of his frank and brutally honest references, colleagues respected his judgment. At one point after the student left the room in tears, this individual said to me that he wouldn't just write a "feel good" reference for the sake of doing so. As a result, when he recommended people, even if his references contained an element of critical commentary, people sat up and listened to what he had to say about a person. The moral of the story is that soliciting a reference that is positive overall but also balanced with some elements of critical feedback is a much stronger and more credible endorsement of your capabilities than the standard listing of positive yet vague list of adjectives that has come to characterize most reference letters.

In sum, alert your references that you will be submitting their names; request feedback on how they will describe you to future employers, and if possible, seek to use references from credible resources who can present a balanced look at your strengths and possible limitations. As long as the latter attributes are not presented as deal breakers that will automatically rule you out, you will come across in the end as a credible candidate who will be seen in a more realistic light by your prospective employer.

There is one special case I would like to discuss at this point because it might pertain to more than just a handful of the readers of this book. The situation arose from a question a participant recently raised in one of my sessions on testing and interviewing for a new job. During the session, a question was raised about a reference from a bad boss who caused the participant to quit her job at her former company. It should be noted that this individual reported to this unpleasant person for almost nine years. Nevertheless, the former employee was terrified that if prospective employers called this difficult manager for a reference, he would say exceptionally critical things about her. My response to this participant's question explained that she should describe to a potential employer the situation from her perspective and say that her former boss might see things differently.

In reality, it is unlikely that her former boss, no matter how cruel, will say slanderous things about this person for fear of reprisals from the human resources department. Moreover, I told this participant that she should be prepared to answer the more important question as to why she remained in such an abusive relationship at work for so many years. Perhaps it was the need of a paycheck to support her family, but whatever the reason, this situation is more about explaining one's own behavior in an unhappy work setting as opposed to dealing with the possibility of a bad reference.

The State of Reference Checking Today

Today, as hinted above, many companies will not allow their people to provide references on former employees, regardless of how well the latter individual performed on the job. The restrictions on giving references are really nothing new. In fact, for the past thirty years, companies have discouraged their people from speaking to those seeking references on a particular person. The reasons are mostly related to the perceived as well as the real legal liabilities regarding libel and slander for references given on individuals who are not deserving of negative feedback. Of course, most people know only to offer accurate appraisals of former colleagues, but companies are cautious regardless.

This protective policy—generally based on the opinion of either inside or outside counsel—results in almost all references being run through the human resources function of the organization. When a prospective employer calls a company's HR department, they will generally receive very sparse information at best, typically restricted to verifying the employee's dates of employment and little else. Occasionally, position level and even salary might be verified, but nothing that might allow a prospective employer to determine how the person got along with his or her peers or how that same individual performed in the role. Work habits like punctuality and attendance along with productivity are usually out of bounds.

On the other hand, if people at a person's prospective employer have a personal contact at the applicant's former place of work, they might be able to obtain an informal reference "via the grapevine." Most companies frown on their employees providing such information, but it is one way new employers can obtain some kind of record or trace on candidates under consideration for hire. If you know a person at a previous place of work who would be willing to vouch for you, even if discouraged by formal company policy from giving a reference, include that person on your resume. As we will discuss below, it is important to prepare that person ahead of time so that he or she isn't surprised when asked to discuss your previous performance.

It is also possible to be proactive about references by using networking sites, like LinkedIn, which allows those who post on the site to list their recommendations from colleagues and friends. As you prepare for your job search, you can contact former bosses and coworkers along with customers and others who might have had contact with you through such activities as professional associations. A varied list of references on your LinkedIn site is easy to access, and it can mitigate the above-mentioned problems of trying to extract a reference from a reluctant employer who is restricted by official HR policy. If you go this route, again, make sure you have a representative sample of people who will speak in your behalf. If possible, try to encourage these people to provide pithy examples about your capabilities as opposed to broad generalizations like "Shirley is a hard worker" or "Tom is a friendly guy." Examples citing projects completed or results achieved are much preferred.

Keep People Informed

Many people simply submit a list of references to their future employers and leave it at that. Even if you go through the motions of seeking feedback on how you will be portrayed by a reference, the process doesn't stop there. Touch base from time to time with your references. By all means, let them know where you were interviewed and what kind of timetable you are working on to seek a new position with a prospective employer. You don't want one of your references getting a call and having that person act surprised or be unprepared to speak on your behalf. Just letting someone know that they might expect a call, and better yet, who exactly might be calling, will forewarn your reference and make for a more informed conversation.

Furthermore, it is a good idea to ask your references if they know anybody at the company where you will be interviewed. They might be able to put in a good word for you even before you make an onsite visit for a round of initial job interviews. Arriving at a prospective employer with a good word in your behalf is an added advantage to say the least. Perhaps, if your references aren't aware of anyone at the company, they might know something about the organization. The perspective your references bring will be very helpful as you plan your day of interviews. Tips about dressing properly in light of the company's culture or just little tidbits heard via the grapevine can provide you with useful data.

Regardless, you want to make sure everyone is up to date on your job search activities. Communicating with your references should be done through the mode that is most convenient for them. Certain people will appreciate a quick phone call or voicemail informing them of your progress along with the possibility that they might be called to serve as one of your references. For other people, email is the preferred mode of communication. Furthermore, for those who are busy, a short one or two-line message will suffice. In the case of those who enjoy a lot of detail, a longer email message will probably be appreciated. The bottom line is just as you don't want any surprises, show the same courtesy to those who you have asked to serve as your references for future employment.

Show Appreciation for Their Efforts

Most of this chapter is nothing more than good common sense, but the value of references should not be underestimated even though many companies don't seek them given what we said earlier about the scarcity of information provided by former employers. For those people who are called, and who, in turn, take the time to offer a reference, you owe them a debt of gratitude. Showing appreciation can take many forms.

For example, you should immediately communicate back to these people about the status of your employment with the company that called them. Thank them formally via email or a handwritten note expressing your gratitude for their time and efforts. In addition, taking these individuals out to lunch is not out of the question if they have the time and inclination to want to join you for a meal. Even a small gift reflecting their preferences is proper (e.g., a bottle of wine, a modest gift certificate, etc.). Perhaps, even more importantly, serve as a reference for them or to any other people you feel comfortable in recommending. The old saying that what goes around comes around is very apt in these situations, and someone who reaches out to help you in a time of need might just require a favor in return at another time in his or her career.

In closing, it is a small world. Most people have spent their careers in a tight-knit community in their chosen line of work. By the time you are more senior and seasoned in your career, you will have built up a lot of contacts. Naturally, you want to avoid burning any bridges behind you because you never know about the future. When all is said and done, being able to generate a ready and viable list of references to speak on your behalf might provide the extra added edge you need to win a job when the competition is fierce and the stakes are high.

CHAPTER TEN

Turning the Tables

So much of this book is written from the perspective of the job seeker who is sitting on the other side of the desk being evaluated in interviews or working away at a terminal, completing a battery of online testing tools. Even in requesting references from your previous colleagues, you are in the position of being subjected to some kind of an evaluation process. In short, much of what transpires in the job search process causes the candidate to be reactive as opposed to proactive, at least with respect to the evaluative component of the employment process. Regardless, there is no question that the hiring process places the candidate in a role where judgments are being rendered about that person, which will hopefully lead to a favorable outcome in the form of a job offer.

At the same time, it behooves the job applicant to take notice of his or her future surroundings in order to determine if this is the best possible fit for his or her skills and abilities along with his or her needs and interests. Therefore, in this penultimate (now there's a big word to improve your vocabulary) chapter of the book, I suggest a more proactive approach in terms of performing your own assessment of the people and surroundings where you will hopefully be spending a significant amount of time. This means shedding the perception that you are a passive player in this process at the mercy of your prospective employer (now, that's an alliteration).

Earlier, information was offered about using the Internet to prepare for the interviews you will be having at a potential place of work, but in this last chapter, we go even further in suggesting ways to be proactive and gain a more equal footing with a prospective employer; we recommend turning the tables on those people evaluating you. In order to assume a more active role, you have to know exactly what you will be looking for and evaluating during the job search process. The ensuing sections of this chapter provide some guidance and suggestions for making the most of your time onsite at an organization. Remember: the employment decision is a two-way street.

Evaluating the Physical Surroundings of the Organization

What might not seem so obvious to you and most people is the simple act of surveying the physical surroundings of the place you might be working in the future. How many times have we all simply walked into a workplace and went about our business without bothering to look around and take note of our environment? Yet if you really take the time to look carefully, you can observe a lot of interesting things that might be very helpful in deciding if this is a place where you want to spend a considerable number of your waking hours.

For example, the physical location of the company along with the structure of the building can be very telling. Is the company located in a beautiful new office park or tall, downtown high-rise building? Or are the surroundings dingy and the office rather utilitarian? The latter is not necessarily a bad thing. In its early days, Wal-Mart's headquarters in Bentonville, Arkansas, allegedly contained a number of military-style Quonset huts. The company was focused on making money through sales and saving money with modest overhead expenses. In other instances, an expensive piece of real estate and a designer office building might be saying something about the image the company wishes to project to the public, or in certain instances, it can be a statement about the owner's ego. You won't have the answer to any of these questions until you dig deeper, but you're on the right track.

The company parking lot is worth a look around. If you arrive at an early hour—say before 7 a.m.—is the lot full of cars? What about after hours, are there a lot of cars still parked in the lot? In addition, what is the general parking arrangement? Is it first come first served? Are there assigned parking spots? Do the bigwigs have reserved spots to park their cars? And also, if those executive parking spaces are full, what kinds and models of cars occupy those spots? Finally, in general, what about the other cars in the lot? Are they expensive? Are they the latest model cars? Or are the cars older and reflective of a sampling of tastes and possible incomes?

Once you've surveyed your surroundings, let's look at a few other important indicators. For example, who greets you? Is there someone at the reception desk? What is the tone of voice and demeanor of that person? Friendly? Helpful? Welcoming? Does someone offer to hang your coat or store your luggage if you have traveled from out of town? Did anyone ask about a cup of coffee or something to drink? Or perhaps that individual is frowning or indifferent or even distant and cold, or worse, downright unfriendly and inhospitable.

Besides the person who greets you, the other people that you have observed and encountered, what are they like? Are they talking to one another and smiling? Or might they be serious and task-focused? Obviously, there are advantages and disadvantages to each, but you need to think if you'd be a good fit for such an environment. If you're very social, and people rarely look up from their desks, this might not be a terribly satisfying place to spend your day. On the other hand, if you are quiet and reserved and just want to get down to business, this might just be like heaven for you.

As you walk through the organization during your day of interviews and appointments, what do you see? Is the office equipped with state-of-the-art technology? Is this important to you and your line of work, or does it not matter? What about the dress code? Is it formal, requiring a suit and tie for everyone? Or perhaps it's highly informal all the way down to blue jeans and flip-flops? Again, neither style of dress is inherently good or bad, it all depends on what you've been used to in the past, and more importantly, what you would prefer in the future. It is also worth watching to see if there are different rules for different groups. Are people with a considerable amount of direct customer contact such as the sales and marketing teams required to dress in a more formal fashion, while back office employees in information technology or accounts payable and receivable are allowed to dress any way they want? Along this same line of thought, do you sense that certain departments or functions are given greater preferential treatment? Are you able to observe any outward signs of favoritism between various functions?

One thing that I like to observe is what is hanging on the walls. Is there expensive artwork? What kind of a statement is that making about the company? What about motivational posters? In many places of work, there is the company credo or mission statement laminated and plastered on every wall. As we will discuss later, many companies post their corporate philosophy, but unfortunately, that's where it stops. You will want to determine if the company truly lives by the values it espouses and displays conspicuously on its walls.

Finally, what about the office space allotted to the employees? Do people work in individual offices? Please note that this is likely a thing of the past with the exception of the more senior managers in the organization. If the company has cubicles, are they quiet and allow for privacy? Can you easily hear people speaking on their phones, giving the impression that there is no privacy? In addition, how are the cubicles decorated? Does the company allow for individuality, or is it a sterile environment with no family pictures allowed? At the other extreme, are the cubicles crammed with toys? This could include basketball hoops and putting greens along with collections of model trucks or even collector items like dolls and figurines, to name just a few.

By now, you get the idea that everything is fair game from the stacks and piles of paper you observe on people's desks to the clean workplaces signaling an electronic environment and a paperless office. You can also gain some insight about the organization by the reading materials on the coffee table in the waiting area. By being a good detective, you can learn a lot about a company even before you have your first interview. It is a good idea to take a few notes as well.

Remember, the people at the company who talk to you and interview you will probably be taking copious notes for their own reference.

Evaluating Your Prospective Coworkers

Of course, a building is just a building no matter how modern or rundown its outward appearance. The key to any organization is the kind of people who work there. After all, this will have the greatest impact on your day-to-day level of morale and job satisfaction. Clearly, there is no way you will get to meet every employee at the company, unless it is relatively small, between ten and fifty people. Regardless, many studies that focus on employee morale show that a person's satisfaction or dissatisfaction with his or her job is closely linked to that individual's relationship with his or her immediate supervisor. In short, if you like your boss (as well as your other colleagues at work), you will probably like your job. Conversely, having a bad boss for whatever reason will adversely impact your subsequent experience with the company.

The same principles someone like me as a business psychologist uses in evaluating potential new hires can be turned back on a prospective employer to obtain meaningful and useful results. For example, all of the parties involved in the selection process, to include the candidate and the hiring manager as well as the representatives from human resources, want to put their best foot forward. In a way, the situation is akin to a first date, where both parties are on their best behavior. As in any dating situation, if either or both parties want a second date, which in the employment setting might mean a second round of interviews or possibly even a job offer on the spot, certain facts of life will apply. Specifically, most employers, like the candidates they interview will tend to deny their weaknesses and claim strengths that might be an exaggeration of sorts. For example, a prospective boss who emphasizes over and over that he is participative might not be as collaborative as he proclaims. Or the woman who professes one too many times that she is not a micromanager is probably a person who supervises too closely.

In sum, listen cautiously to what people are telling you and evaluate that information very carefully before accepting a job offer.

One reason you will be hearing these kinds of statements about styles and approaches, which are inconsistent with a person's everyday behavior once on the job, is that people have been told by their fellow employees, for example, that they are unilateral or controlling, and they wish to deny such accusations because it casts them in an unfavorable light. By saying who they're not or claiming to be someone who is not reflective of their real selves, they are trying to woo the candidate to come work for the organization.

Using a specific example, suppose a prospective supervisor tells you that he has enjoyed seeing the people who have reported to him advance in their careers, without trying to put the person on the spot, you might ask for a couple of examples of people who have been promoted and what that particular manager did to get the individual ready to take the next step in his or her career. Similarly, a collaborative manager should be asked exactly what he or she does to encourage the input and participation of other people.

Also listen carefully to the words and pronouns the interviewer uses, especially if you will be working closely with that person. For example, do you hear a lot of "I" statements? Does the person credit other people when discussing successful projects and achievements? What is the other person's overall tone of voice? Are there more positive-sounding statements coming from the individual, or do you hear a lot of criticisms about other people? Is the interviewer prone to blaming others when things go wrong, or does that person take full responsibility for his or her role in various setbacks and disappointments? Remember, if a person talks critically about other people, you can bet that same individual will also probably talk negatively about you at some point during your employment with the organization.

If your gut tells you that the person who will be your immediate supervisor is not someone you would want to be around for extended periods of time, it is best to back out now. Also, listen carefully to how other people characterize not only your boss, but also your potential work team. Are they described in favorable terms? Is there veiled criticism or jealously about how they are treated in the organization? And if the latter is the case, you need to figure out why this is occurring. The amount of direct contact you will have with your coworkers should moderate your initial reactions. For example, if you don't necessarily like these people, but you will be traveling 75 percent of the time, this might prove to be a moot point. On the other hand, if extensive day-to-day contact is required, you better make sure this is a group you would want to wake up in the morning relatively excited to see.

Assessing the Culture: What's really valued?

As mentioned earlier, many organizations have a penchant for mission statements. They typically hire high-priced outside consultants to help them craft such statements, and then in an attempt to encourage buy-in on the part of the employees, the values are framed and placed on every available area of white space on the company's office walls. While this is admittedly a little cynical in terms of my take on most corporate mission statements, very few organizations actually practice what they preach. In fact, in many instances, quite the opposite is true.

For instance, how many companies boast of valuing their employees but have been through countless rounds of layoffs, often terminating people around the holiday season at the end of the calendar year in order to gain better tax advantages by their actions? We have seen organizations preach the importance of customer service, but after all of their sermons have been said and done, they still take their time in responding to requests for help. Clearly, it's hard to determine the hypocrisy regarding the discrepancies of what is practiced and what is preached, especially based on a single visit to a company's office. At the same time, it is possible to look closer at a company's culture.

On the positive side of the ledger, companies that value their employees typically do things to show that their words and deeds are consistent. One place to look is the company cafeteria if the organization is large enough. Providing a wide variety of food along with healthy choices to eat at lunch or during breaks is a sure sign of concern for a company's employees. Related to the notion of keeping employees healthy and fit, does the company have an exercise facility onsite? Or do they provide free memberships to nearby health clubs, or at the very least, offer a subsidized rate?

One of the best ways to learn more about what's really valued in an organization is to ask on what grounds you will be evaluated by your manager. Ask for a sample form used in the annual performance review process. It is also a good idea to ask your future coworkers, and in particular, the supervisors and managers, about who gets promoted. What are their outstanding qualities? Why were these people picked ahead of their peers? If, for example, a company advocates having a diverse workforce, but the people who have been promoted over the last couple of years have had a marginally acceptable track record for promoting minorities and women, but their sales or production numbers were strong, then there's your answer. In sum, what is typically measured and rewarded is what gets attention in the office and not what is hanging by a hook in a picture frame on the wall.

Company culture, of course, goes beyond mission statements and the influence of outside consultants. The formality or informality of the dress code says a lot about a company's culture. But again, the following tale might serve as a word or two of caution about misinterpreting the meaning of "every day is casual day."

Many years ago, we worked with a client company that was one of the "pioneers" in casual dress. Long before everyone came to work looking like they were on vacation, suits and ties were banned by this organization. At the same time, the company fostered an incredibly competitive and even cutthroat work environment—not necessarily noticeable during an initial visit. But after spending time at their offices, it became apparent that people tried to outdo each other with their designer blue jeans and T-shirts along with other expensive casual wear. Hence, simply looking at the clothes on people's backs as compared to other companies at the time, one might think of the place as laidback and relaxed. In this case what was valued by the company was one-upmanship and political infighting as opposed to a relaxed atmosphere that encouraged free thinking and creativity.

In general, all companies have a culture, just as all families are unique in some way. The strength of the culture varies. In companies where pretty much anything goes and all different kinds of behavior are accepted, it will be easier to be yourself. In those instances, however, where the company's culture is rather rigidly defined, you need to make sure that your attitudes and behavior are consistent with what's valued and rewarded. If not, you will prove to be a poor fit for the company and likely want to leave your job sooner rather than later.

Too often, prospective new hires focus on the usual suspects concerning pay and benefit packages, to include vacation time and family leave policies. While these are important components of any job, they must be considered in the context of a company's culture. For example, "family-friendly" is one of the most oft-used buzzwords you hear when a company tries to sell itself to potential recruits. Typically, the term means allowing for a work/life balance for employees so that they can enjoy their families, and in particular, are available to attend after-hours activities for their children such as sporting events along with plays and concerts. All good so far. But what happens to those who try to take advantage of these family-friendly policies? Do they impede their career advancement by taking an extended maternity leave or caring for a relative or elderly parent? How is the father who tries to leave early to attend his daughter's soccer practices regarded? If the company espouses one doctrine but clearly rewards employees with salary hikes and promotions for doing something else, then there is a fundamental disconnect between the so-called culture at the company and its proposed set of values.

Determining the Right Fit and the Perils of a Bad Fit

No matter how badly you want a job, you must be honest with yourself about your ability to survive and thrive inside of an organization where you and the culture are a poor fit. Furthermore, locating a place of employment where you are in sync with the values and reward structure of the organization will make returning to work all that much more enjoyable. The devil is in the details so to speak, so that by digging deep, you will uncover the factors that will make the company a suitable fit for your talents and interests and is likely to save you a lot of unhappiness.

The nature of our firm's work is to assess the suitability of prospective employees before one of our client companies make those individuals a final job offer. While we are in business at the behest of our clients—after all they pay the bills—we also think that it is in the candidate's best interest to make sure the job is the right fit. We say to candidates, for example, what happens if you get this job and you are not a good fit for the role or the company? What will you do with this job if six to nine months later you are asked to resign or you choose to do so before being asked to leave?

Once again, as we stated several times before in this book, we ask potential candidates, are you going to list the short-term job on your resume and then spend the majority of every subsequent job interview with other prospective employers trying to explain away your six to nine months with the company? Or perhaps, even riskier, you might decide to leave this short-term stint off your resume entirely and hope no one finds out about it. But if it is discovered through an Internet search or some other means that you did have this six to nine month position, then what will you do? Likely, you will be called into the HR department at your next place of work and be asked to resign for falsifying your resume. Not a lot of good choices here. In the end, making sure you are comfortable with the values and demands of your next job is critical. Now I realize that in today's tough economy, having the choice of being perfectly happy and content with your next job is idealistic, and perhaps, not even very realistic. Moreover, if your finances are being stretched and you need health insurance, looking at all of the niceties just described doesn't count for much. Nevertheless, even if you feel that you have to "settle" at your next place of employment, make sure that at least your most important criteria for wanting to stay at a particular job are met.

This might mean sacrificing a few preferences such as position title or salary level. If the potential to attain the level of job that you had prior to this is within reach, or you will be able to earn back your former salary within a reasonable length of time, then it might well be worth accepting a job offer should one be forthcoming. On other issues such as overnight travel, you have to be the judge, especially in light of the other demands in your life like family, community activities, and commitments.

At the same time, you don't want to compromise your core values. One thing we do not recommend is accepting a vague promise about certain important conditions that are unlikely to materialize. Often, these poorly defined promises might involve being promoted within a specified period of time or changes in your job demands like less overnight travel or the hiring of extra help or additional resources to lighten your workload. Unless these future commitments are verified in writing, be careful. And even in those instances where something is written on paper, subsequent business conditions from failing finances to new ownership in a merger or acquisition could wipe out any past promises or commitments.

At the conclusion of the day, only you can make the final call as to whether a particular job is a good fit. The more you do your homework and, of course, observe your prospective employer during the hiring process, the better equipped you will be in making an informed decision about your future. You have many of the tools at this point, so let's land that right job!

CLOSING REMARKS

Putting It All Together

This book, while not intended to be the final word on job hunting strategies for those over forty, will hopefully help those who are in need of assistance in dealing with the painful loss of a job and are looking to reengage in the workforce. As mentioned at the beginning of the book, there are several ways to approach the information on the preceding pages. You can read the book cover to cover from beginning to end, or you might decide to read only selected parts.

If you are recently out of work, you might need time to do inventory on your situation and consider ways to keep active and busy while making productive use of your time. On the other hand, you might be contemplating the notions of being a business owner. Entrepreneurship is a popular topic today, but as I said earlier, it is not for everybody, and unless you possess certain innate qualities, this can be a very risky road to travel, especially if you are putting your own money (as you probably will) into your new venture. In general, anyone considering spending their own hard-earned and likely scarce financial resources on activities like starting a business, buying a franchise, or even returning to school for an expensive degree, look carefully before you leap.

For those individuals at various stages during their job search, to include preparing a resume or getting ready to take a battery of online tests or even going for a round of interviews, you might be better advised to read Part II of this book ahead of anything else. The advice and tips contained in this section are truly views from the other side of the desk. With over thirty years of experience in advising companies on how to select the best qualified candidates, my previous work experience can offer a number of helpful hints as well as provide concrete examples of strategies that work and those that don't. With increasing numbers of people competing for fewer and fewer job openings, companies have the luxury of being picky. They also have at their disposal the latest research and technology to screen applicants quickly. Without any kind of preparation on your part, your chances for landing a job will be diminished.

It is also advisable to use this book as a ready reference. Make notes in the margins and reread various parts that are of particular interest to you. While eBooks are becoming more and more popular, having a hardcopy in front of you for notes and easy reference mitigates the desire to retain the book as part of your electronic library.

For those who elect to read the book from start to finish, the flow of the book makes sense. You need to understand your prospects in today's competitive economic environment. The Three A's (age, appearance, and attitude) are critical even if they reek of political incorrectness. No one is doing you any favors if you are over forty by dancing around these topics or trying to minimize their impact on your chances of gaining re-employment. Also worth addressing is the idea of seeking outside help and assistance, whether in the form of taking legal action against your former employer or turning to a trained mental health professional or career counselor for treatment and guidance.

Staying active and productive is a key to keeping your mind focused and sharp as well as allowing you to interact with many other people. While some of the people you mingle with might be in the same boat as you, by showing off your talents and abilities in any number of venues, you could find yourself impressing exactly the right person who might connect you to an excellent job opportunity.

It also helps to assess your current skills and determine whether or not you need extra training or education to fill in any gaps. An entire chapter is devoted to the attributes employers want in employees. This is based on thirty years of consulting experience, and the list, while not exhaustive, should help you benchmark where your strengths and weaknesses reside.

Once you've done your prep work and assessed your options, to include being your own boss or taking a chance and changing careers altogether, the next step involves finding the right job for you. As we discussed earlier, there is plenty of free (and helpful) advice on what to do with your resume. Unfortunately, the amount of hard data or scientific research on the topic is scant; hence, much is left to old wives' tales and hearsay. Advice on excluding identifying information about your age abounds. There are also gurus who will tell you to keep your resume to one page and no more. The right langauge is also important as the software used to process the reams of resumes sent for every job opening searches for words and phrases which distinguish qualified candidates.

Testing and interviewing, always popular and frequently used in the past, are now even more commonplace as companies attempt to weed out unqualified candidates to make their work easier and more efficient. Navigating these two popularly used employment tools is not easy, and while this book is not about "gaming" the system, there are steps you can take to avoid being disqualified when in fact you would be a good fit for the job. Several approaches are discussed, which have achieved an almost fad-like aura about them, and if you are unprepared to handle them, your chances for advancing in the hiring process will be limited. In particular, we are talking about everything from Internet-administered personality tests to behaviorial-based interview strategies. Finally, we add a brief word about references.

In our closing comments about the employment process, we suggest that you turn the tables on your prospective employers and play "psychologist." Observe your potential surroundings, looking at everything from the parking lot to the pictures on the wall. Study the people at the company and how they behave. Finally, examine the culture of the company for consistencies or inconsistencies between what is rewarded and what is said in the organization's well-publicized mission statement. In short, if the words on the wall don't match the actions in the office, then think hard about joining the company. Ultimately, this book should help you find a job that is a good landing spot. Whether your primary needs are for variety and challenge or financial security, you must feel comfortable in your new role, or you will be rereading this book sooner than you would like.

While the hiring process is designed in many ways to make you feel powerless and out of control, you have more influence than you might think. Use that influence to make this time in your life worthwhile and productive beyond just the need to survive emotionally and financially. As noted before, unemployment is a full-time job. For better or worse, we measure so much of our self-worth by what we do outside of the home. Therefore, you want to have every possible advantage in making your job search effective and, ultimately, a satisfying experience. Remember, every one of you has been a success at some point in your life, and believe me, you will succeed again. Don't give up and let your worst fears gain the upper hand. In the end, you will find the kind of opportunity that will allow you to meet your requirements as you continue along in your career until you decide that it is time to put the world of work behind you and retire.

ACKNOWLEDGEMENTS

This book would not have been possible without the help of many people. While my work places me on the other side of the desk from those seeking jobs, it became very noticeable over the last 15 years that many job seekers – especially those over 40 – had experienced long periods of unemployment as they sought to become gainfully re-employed in the job market. Toward that end, I initially began volunteering my time with various not-for-profit groups where job seekers gathered for both advice and support. The first group that allowed me to offer help on job search strategies and interviewing skills was the Career Resource Center in Lake Forest, Illinois. Under the capable and positive leadership of their Executive Director, Jan Leahey, this organization has managed to lift the hopes and spirits of many out-of-work and over-40 individuals who were experiencing the pain and frustration along with the all-too-often feelings of humiliation that accompany prolonged periods of unemployment.

Besides the Career Resource Center in Lake Forest, I have also had the opportunity to address on many occasions audiences of unemployed individuals serviced by the Barrington Career Center in Barrington, Illinois, now called the Career Place. The many professionals and volunteers affiliated with that organization perform wonderful work as well. Another group that I have had the good fortune to address is the St. Hubert's Network based in Hoffman Estates, Illinois.

In the private sector dealing with those in transition, I have enjoyed a long and satisfying relationship with the former SSP Group, now part of the BPI Group, North America. In particular, I would like to acknowledge my long association with Paul Schneider, one of the group's founders, who has been a friend and colleague for over 25 years. Paul was also helpful in reviewing parts of the manuscript. In addition, Duncan Ferguson who has worked with Paul and the other people at SSP BPI has been a great friend and colleague who has allowed me to speak to his groups of unemployed professionals in HR and finance to name a few.

The professional presentation of this book would not have been possible without the careful and conscientious work of Molly Webber, who painstakingly proofread every page of the manuscript. Molly juggled her work with me between her additional work obligations at Northwestern University Memorial Hospital as well as in between her classes at college. She is a truly hard working and committed young woman who will prove to be a success in whatever field in which she endeavors to work. The publishing professionals at Xlibris also deserve a word of thanks and appreciation for all of their fine efforts.

The team at Stephen A. Laser Associates merits a special word of thanks for granting me the time to work on this project and also address the above-mentioned groups. In particular, Joe Banasiak and Pamela Webber (Molly's mom in case you couldn't guess) have both been generous with their comments and encouragement. They are true professionals who exemplify the competencies identified in this book as distinguishing exceptional employees.

Clearly, this book would not have possible without the encouragement of my family. My daughters Carolyn and Eleanor keep me in check with their good-natured kidding along with their love and support. I am also grateful to all of the other "children" in my life who lift my spirits. This includes, Elliot and Dana and Lauren and David along with Amanda and Hannah, and of course, my adorable grandchildren, Solomon and Benjamin. Finally, to Laurie who has been the love of my life and true soul mate, I owe an incalculable debt that can never be repaid. She provides me with inspiration and love, and most important of all, a great sense of humor and a never-ending sense of perspective.

In closing, the views and opinions contained in this book are purely mine and as such I take complete responsibility for them.

Stephen A. Laser, Ph. D
Chicago, Illinois (July, 2011)

CPSIA information can be obtained at www.ICGtesting.com
Printed in the USA
LVOW092000191211

260159LV00009B/111/P